Edmund Gosse, Thomas Gray

Selected Poems

Edmund Gosse, Thomas Gray

Selected Poems

ISBN/EAN: 9783744709750

Printed in Europe, USA, Canada, Australia, Japan

Cover: Foto ©Thomas Meinert / pixelio.de

More available books at **www.hansebooks.com**

Clarendon Press Series

GRAY

SELECTED POEMS

EDITED BY

EDMUND GOSSE
CLARK LECTURER IN ENGLISH LITERATURE AT THE UNIVERSI
OF CAMBRIDGE

Oxford
AT THE CLARENDON PRESS
1885

[*All rights reserved*]

PREFACE.

THE text followed in the present edition is that of the Collected Works of Gray in prose and verse, in four volumes, edited by myself, and published by Messrs. Macmillan in 1884. In preparing that text, I adhered strictly, whenever it was possible, to Gray's revised collection of his poems, corrected by himself in 1768, and in other cases to his own autograph, or to early copies of that autograph. I desire to thank Messrs. Macmillan for the permission to reprint several of my notes from this edition of 1884, and for the authority to base the introductory memoir in the present volume on the life of Gray which I prepared for them from original sources in 1882, in the series of 'English Men of Letters,' edited by Mr. John Morley, M.P. Except in one or two cases, where I had new material to guide me, the present Life may be considered as a reduction of that biography.

In forming my selection, I have given all the pieces which are characteristic of the main features of Gray's genius as an English poet. I have omitted the dramatic fragment called *Agrippina*, the unfinished didactic poem on *The Alliance of Education and Government*, the slight

PREFACE.

and humorous pieces, and most of the translations. The only exceptions to the latter omission are two paraphrases of Propertius and of Dante, which I was the first to discover and print, the excellence and novelty of which seem to excuse their admission here.

E. G.

29 DELAMERE TERRACE, LONDON:
October, 1884.

CONTENTS.

	PAGE
LIFE AND POEMS OF GRAY	1

POEMS.

ODE TO THE SPRING	29
ODE ON THE DEATH OF A FAVOURITE CAT, Drowned in a Tub of Gold Fishes	31
ODE ON A DISTANT PROSPECT OF ETON COLLEGE	32
HYMN TO ADVERSITY	36
THE PROGRESS OF POESY. A Pindaric Ode	38
THE BARD. A Pindaric Ode	42
THE FATAL SISTERS. An Ode	48
THE DESCENT OF ODIN	51
THE TRIUMPHS OF OWEN	54
ELEGY WRITTEN IN A COUNTRY CHURCH-YARD	56
A LONG STORY	61
THE INSTALLATION ODE	66
SONNET ON THE DEATH OF RICHARD WEST	70
HYMN TO IGNORANCE. A Fragment	71
STANZAS TO MR. RICHARD BENTLEY	72
ODE ON THE PLEASURE ARISING FROM VICISSITUDE. Fragment	73
EPITAPH ON MRS. JANE CLERKE	76
EPITAPH ON A CHILD	76
SKETCH OF HIS OWN CHARACTER Written in 1761, and found in one of his Pocket-Books	77
EPITAPH ON SIR WILLIAM WILLIAMS	77
THE DEATH OF HOEL. An Ode. Selected from the Gododin	78
CARADOC	79

	PAGE
CONAN	79
IMPROMPTU. Suggested by a View, in 1766, of the Seat and Ruins of a Deceased Nobleman, at Kingsgate, Kent	80
AMATORY LINES	81
SONG	81
FROM PROPERTIUS	82
FROM DANTE	85

NOTES.

Ode on the Spring	92
Ode on the Death of a Favourite Cat	93
Ode on a Distant Prospect of Eton College	94
Hymn to Adversity	97
The Progress of Poesy	98
The Bard	104
The Fatal Sisters	109
The Descent of Odin	110
The Triumphs of Owen	112
Elegy written in a Country Church-Yard	113
A Long Story	120
The Installation Ode	122
Sonnet	124
Hymn to Ignorance	125
Stanzas to Mr. Richard Bentley	126
Ode on Vicissitude	126
Epitaph on Mrs. Jane Clerke	128
Epitaph on a Child	128
Sketch of his own Character	128
Epitaph on Sir William Williams	128
Welsh Fragments	129
Impromptu	129
Amatory Lines	129
Song	129
From Propertius	130
From Dante	132

LIFE AND POEMS OF GRAY.

THOMAS GRAY was born on the 26th of December, 1716, in his father's house in Cornhill. There is some slight reason to suppose that he was a connexion of the family of Baron Gray of Gray in Forfarshire, but practically he belonged to the lower middle class. His father, Philip Gray, born July 27th, 1676, was the son of Thomas Gray, a successful city merchant, who left a fortune of £10,000. Philip Gray married Dorothy Antrobus, who, with her sister Mary, kept a milliner's shop in the city. Of twelve children born to Philip and Dorothy Gray, Thomas, the future poet, was the only one who survived infancy; he would have succumbed to the convulsions which carried off the others, if his mother had not courageously opened a vein in his throat with a pair of scissors.

His father alternately ignored and illtreated his mother and himself, and he was early taken away from home, and brought up at Burnham, in Bucks, by his mother's brother, Robert Antrobus, who died early in 1729. The boy was sent to Eton in 1727, at his mother's expense; and at this school he formed his celebrated friendship with Horace Walpole (1717-1797), who was slightly younger than himself, and with Richard West, the son of a promising Lord Chancellor of Ireland of the same name. A fourth friend was Thomas Ashton, and these four boys formed a 'quadruple alliance' at Eton, until, in 1734, Gray and Ashton proceeded to Cambridge and West to Oxford. Gray was admitted as a pensioner of Pembroke Hall, but very soon after, on the 3rd of July, went over as a fellow-commoner to Peterhouse. Meanwhile West, who showed great aptitude for literature, was at Christ Church, Oxford, and the earliest letters of Gray's which have been preserved are addressed to him there.

In February 1735 Mrs. Dorothy Gray submitted a case to the eminent civilian John Audley, in which she stated that for nearly thirty years, that is to say, for the whole of her married life, she had received no support from her husband, but had depended entirely on the receipts of the shop kept by herself and her sister, and 'almost provided everything for her son, whilst at Eton School, and now he is at Peter-House in Cambridge.' The personal cruelty of her husband too, seems to have been excessive, and it can only be supposed that he was mad. She found, however, no legal remedy, and we do not know what sequel there was to this extraordinary application.

Meanwhile Gray, Horace Walpole and Ashton were together at Cambridge from the spring of 1735 to the winter of 1738. Early in 1736 they simultaneously made their first appearance in print in a volume of Latin hymeneals on the marriage of Frederic, Prince of Wales, entitled *Gratulatio Academiae Cantabrigiensis*, and published in folio by the University. A year later Gray contributed another exercise in hexameters, *Luna Habitabilis*, to the second volume of the *Musae Etonenses*. His letters to West, whom he addressed under the name of Favonius, are the chief indication we possess of his condition of mind during these years, and they display him to us already as fantastic, melancholy, learned beyond his years, and possessed of great refinement of feeling. In his vacations he haunted Burnham Beeches, in the neighbourhood of his uncle's house in Buckinghamshire, and it was in August 1736 that he wrote his famous letter on those 'very reverend vegetables,' which has led to their shade becoming classic ground. At Burnham, also, in 1737, he made the acquaintance and enjoyed the company of the venerable tragic dramatist, Thomas Southerne (1660-1746).

At Cambridge he became increasingly unhappy as his progress compelled him more and more to give up his time to mathematics, which he detested. His third term seems to have been absolute wretchedness to him. In December 1736 he declined to take degrees, and threatened to leave college, but this determination seems to have been overruled. Walpole left Cambridge at the death of his mother, in August 1737, and Gray became extremely solitary and dejected, and appeared, even to his friend West, who was himself a bookworm, to neglect all bodily exercise to excess. Gray had, however, by this time become an admirable scholar. Some of his best Latin poems date from 1738, and he was now beginning to translate classical passages into excellent English verse. In September 1738 he left Cambridge, and spent a year of idleness in his mother's house. He then accepted an invitation from Horace Walpole to accompany him on the grand tour, and the friends left England on the 29th of March, 1739.

Gray's visit to the Continent was the only one he ever made, but it lasted three years, and left an indelible mark on his tastes and character. The companions landed at Calais, visited various towns in Picardy, and arrived in Paris on the 9th of April. Their stay in Paris lasted nearly three months, during which time they moved in the best diplomatic and literary society, the son of the English prime minister being welcomed everywhere. Among the interesting Frenchmen with whom they consorted was the Abbé Prévôt d'Exiles (1697–1763), author of *Manon Lescaut*, and Crébillon *fils*. Walpole's cousins, the Conways, and Lord Holdernesse, showed them a great deal of hospitality, and they made excursions by moonlight to Versailles and Chantilly. On the 1st of June, in company with Henry Conway, they proceeded to Rheims, where·they lodged for three months; in September they passed on to Dijon and Lyons, which latter town was their head-quarters for six weeks. From Lyons they took an excursion into Savoy and Switzerland, and it was on this occasion that Gray became first impressed by the grandeur of mountain scenery.

On their return they found a letter waiting for them from Sir Robert Walpole, in which he desired his son to go on at once to Italy. Accordingly, in November, and armed against the cold with 'muffs, hoods and masks of beaver, fur boots and bearskins,' they crossed the Alps and reached Turin. The passage of the mountains had greatly charmed Gray, in an age when the sublime in Nature was disregarded or regarded only with horror. In a letter to West he used this phrase, which has become classic :—'not a precipice, not a torrent, not a cliff, but is pregnant with religion and poetry.' They passed through Genoa, Piacenza and Parma, to Bologna, whence, after a short stay, they descended to Florence, and took up their abode in the house of the English Resident, Sir Horace Mann. This was their home, with certain intervals, for fifteen months. Gray plunged into society less than Horace Walpole did, and occupied himself mainly with the study of painting, architecture and music, on which subjects he made copious collections of notes.

On the news of the death of Pope Clement XII, the friends went hurriedly to Rome, in March 1740, to be present at the coronation of his successor. This, however, was long delayed, and they found Rome very tedious 'after sunset.' In June they could wait for the cardinals no longer, and they set out for Terracina, Capua, and Naples. After exploring the vicinity of the Bay of Naples, they returned to Rome, but finding that still no Pope was elected, they determined to return to Florence. They had now been absent from home and habitually thrown upon one another for entertainment during nearly fifteen months, and their friendship had hitherto shown no abatement. But they had arrived at that point of familiarity when a little disagreement is sufficient to produce a quarrel. There was, however, no distinct breach for a year or more. They took up their abode again in Florence, and Gray began a Latin poem, *De Principiis Cogitandi*, the fragment of which— for he never finished it—is the longest of his poetical writings.

On the 24th of April 1741, Gray and Walpole left Florence; they passed on to Bologna, and to Reggio, where the famous quarrel took place which divided them. It is said that Gray discovered Walpole opening a letter addressed to Gray; at all events he broke away from him in a rage, and proceeded alone to Venice. After Gray's death, Walpole, in 1773, took the whole fault upon himself. Much more has been made of this quarrel than it deserves; it rather shows that the habits of mind which led them together were unusually attractive, that they should have lived together, without a quarrel, for nearly three years, in a foreign country and without any other employment than pleasure. In 1744 the breach was healed. Gray in July 1741 left Italy for England. As he crossed the Alps he inscribed in the album of the Fathers of the Grande Chartreuse his famous Latin *Alcaic Ode*. On the 1st of September he reached home. Walpole returned to England ten days later. Henry Conway tried to suggest a renewal of intimacy between the friends, but Gray's pride had been wounded, and he returned a negative answer of the coldest civility.

Two months after the young man's return to London, his father died of the gout. His last act had been to squander the remainder of his fortune on building a country-house at Wanstead. On the rent of this house, of which she only learned the existence when her husband was dead, and on the ruins of their fortune, Mrs. Gray and her sister Miss Mary Antrobus subsisted in their house in Cornhill for nearly a year. On the 21st of October 1742 their brother-in-law, Jonathan Rogers, died, and they joined their widowed sister in her house at Stoke Poges, Buckinghamshire. During these months they wound up their private business in Cornhill, and disposed of their shop on tolerably advantageous terms; they possessed a competence, and apparently Gray first imagined that the family property would be enough to provide amply for him also. Accordingly he began the study of the law, but not so actively as to exclude literature. His friend Richard West was now declining in health, and he enjoyed Gray's society, to which he had looked forward, only six months. In March 1742 he was obliged to leave town, and to take up his abode at Popes, in Hertfordshire, where, three months later, he died.

The year 1742 was marked in Gray's career as that in which the poetical vein in him ran most freely. Until this time we know of no original pieces of his composed in English verse. His first production of this kind was *Agrippina*, a fragment of a blank verse tragedy, written early in 1742. It was sent to West, who criticised it with such severity that Gray discontinued it, and turned to the paraphrasing of Propertius, with much more skill. He was at this time studying the classics with great assiduity. For instance, in the month of April in this year he read through the *Peloponnesian War*, Anacreon, Aulus Gellius, and the greater part of Pliny and Martial, besides Petrarch in Italian.

West died on the 1st of June, and apparently on the same day Gray went down to visit his uncle and aunt Rogers at Stoke Poges. They lived at West End House, a simple farmstead of two stories, which was to be the poet's home for the rest of his life. A few days after arriving at Stoke, Gray wrote his *Ode to Spring*, which he sent to West, not knowing that he was already dead. When he received this sad news, he was overwhelmed with grief, which found its first relief in a series of beautiful Latin hexameters. Later on, in August of the same year, he wrote his well-known sonnet to Favonius, his favourite name for West ; this is the only sonnet he ever composed. In the same month Gray wrote the *Ode on a Distant Prospect of Eton College*, and the *Ode on Adversity*, and in October is believed to have begun the *Elegy written in a Country Churchyard*. To this year also belongs, in all probability, the very fine paraphrase from Dante which has been recently discovered.

It is obvious therefore that, in consideration of the very small bulk of his entire writings, those which belong to this year, 1742, are very numerous and important. For six years he wrote no more, or very little more, and the odes we have mentioned represent Gray's youthful contribution to English poetry. They were very interesting as being the first distinct protest against the dullness and hardness of Augustan rhyming. It had for sixty years been the fashion to write verse in couplets, and in couplets only. Gray returned to the stanza-form, with richer rhymes, and to an arrangement of each poem which should respond, more or less, to its subject and the treatment of that subject. His language in these earlier odes was not as brilliant as it became later on. He had so steeped his memory in the felicities of the classical poets, and in those of the English poets too, that these early pieces are a mosaic of beauties repeated, adapted or arranged from other sources. This does not, however, militate against Gray's originality, since the images and phrases have all passed through the fuse of his imagination, and become his own. It is not possible to say what was the form of so much of the *Elegy in a Country Churchyard* as was written in 1742, for the poet did not complete it for several years, and has left no record of its earlier condition.

Gray presently found that the family property was very slender, and not enough to support him as well as the three ladies. He took the only course which was open to him, namely, to return to Cambridge, where living was very cheap, and to reside in College, spending his vacations in Stoke Poges. In the winter of 1742 he proceeded to Peterhouse, and taking his Bachelor's degree in Civil Law, was forthwith installed as a resident of that college.

Gray did not become a Fellow of Peterhouse, nor is it explained upon what terms or pretext he took up his abode in it. His letters contain no references to its members, to its governing body, or to its social manners; it is hard to persuade ourselves that he was an inmate of it for fourteen years. On the other hand, his letters were full of the most intimate particulars respecting persons and things at Pembroke College, where he must have mainly lived, even while his nominal residence was Peterhouse. The first years of his life at Cambridge are however very obscure to us. On the 27th of December, 1742, a few days after his arrival at the university, he wrote a letter to Dr. Wharton, which has been preserved, and his fragmentary *Hymn to Ignorance*, Mason tells us, dates from the same time. But after this he entirely disappears from us for two years. We know, however, that during this period, and for some time to ' come, he possessed but few associates. Among these few was Dr. Conyers Middleton (1683–1750), the celebrated Librarian of Trinity, and a few agreeable fellows of Pembroke. Gray certainly found Cambridge excessively dreary, and he humorously declared that she had been pleased to appoint him, 'in preference to so many old servants of her's, who had spent their whole lives in qualifying themselves for the office, Grand Picker of Straws and Push-Pin Player in Ordinary to her Supinity.' In this close atmosphere he wrote no more poetry, but devoted himself for the first five or six years almost exclusively to a study of the whole surviving literature of ancient Greece. He projected a critical text of Strabo; he began to translate the Greek Anthology into Latin verse; he proposed to edit Aristotle on a new plan. His habitual dejection and miserable health prevented him from carrying out any of these designs.

In the winter of 1744 his horizon began to brighten a little. A lady made peace between him and Horace Walpole, and he rejoined in London a Mr. Chute and his nephew, a Mr. Whithead, persons of wealth and taste, with whom he had spent pleasant months in Venice three years before. In the summer of 1745 he had 'serious thoughts' of moving over from Peterhouse to Trinity Hall, but this came to nothing. He was much with Horace Walpole in these years, especially after the latter purchased Strawberry Hill, in May, 1747: for the rest of his life, at least until near the close of it, Gray never spent a long vacation without a visit to Walpole's genteel Gothic cottage. In the summer of 1747 his *Ode on a Distant Prospect of Eton College* was published, without attracting any public attention. A month or two earlier Gray had written his famous *Ode on the Death of Mr. Walpole's Cat*. Meanwhile, as he says in a letter to his Durham friend, Dr. Wharton, 'I have read Pausanias and Athenaeus all through, and Aeschylus again. I am now in Pindar and Lysias, for I take Verse and Prose together, like bread and cheese.'

His house in Cornhill was burned down in May, 1748, and the excitement of this disaster brought about a marked improvement in his spirits. A more lasting fillip was given to them about the same time by the friendship which he formed with William Mason (1725-1797), a scholar of St. John's, who presently entered Pembroke College as a fellow. Mason was the life-long friend, and afterwards the biographer of Gray, whom he imitated, without marked success, in a vast number of odes and elegies. We must, however, acknowledge a debt of gratitude to Mason. He took the sensitive and brooding poet out of himself, he attacked his melancholy, he sustained Gray's nerves by his own physical vigour and versatility. For the first time Gray was now provided with a daily companion who could share his ardent interests in literature. With Walpole to be playful with, and Mason to be serious with, Gray was no longer for the rest of his life exposed to that east wind of solitary wretchedness which had parched him during the first three years of his life at Cambridge.

The disorder and dissipation which prevailed at that time within the University reached a point in 1750 at which further neglect was impossible. The matter was strongly taken up ;

the famous code of Orders and Regulations was passed through the Senate, and a drastic reform was introduced, not before more than twenty persons of good family had been expelled and rusticated. Gray, like the rest of the dons, was interested in these riots and their suppression, and in 1748-49 he wrote, as a contribution to order, his beautiful fragment on *The Alliance of Education and Government*. He found, however, that Montesquieu had forestalled his ideas in *L'Esprit des Lois*, and Gray never carried his poem to a conclusion. It contains some exquisite passages, and was greatly admired by Gibbon.

In Dodsley's celebrated miscellany of fugitive poems, the first three volumes of which appeared in 1748, Gray made his first successful appeal to the public. In the second of these volumes the *Eton Ode* was reprinted, while the *Ode to Spring* and that *On Mr. Walpole's Cat* were first printed, in each case anonymously. Gray sank again into a sort of lethargy, from which he was roused by the somewhat sudden death of his aunt, Mary Antrobus, on the 5th of November, 1749. He was deeply attached to this lady, whom he had been used to, as he says, from infancy, and her death recalled to his memory the *Elegy in a Country Churchyard* which he had begun seven years before, on the occasion of the funeral of his uncle, Jonathan Rogers. He worked upon this poem at Cambridge through the winter of 1749, and put the last touches to it at Stoke Poges on the 12th of June, 1750. He sent it in MS. to Walpole, who was so much delighted with it that he circulated it among his friends, and in this way it reached many readers for whom its author had not intended it. Among these was a Lady Cobham, of Stoke House, who admired it extremely, and was excited to learn that the poet resided within her parish. Gray was proud, and difficult of access, but she sent her niece, Miss Speed, to call upon him, and an acquaintance sprang up which ripened into friendship. These circumstances led, in the summer of 1751, to the composition of the sprightly personal ballad called *A Long Story*, one of the happiest trifles in the language.

Another result of Walpole's indiscretion in circulating copies of the *Elegy* was that Gray was obliged to publish it to prevent spurious editions of it from being foisted upon the public. It was placed in Dodsley's hands and passed through the press with great celerity, appearing on February 16, 1751, as an anonymous quarto pamphlet, entitled *An Elegy wrote in a Country Church-Yard*. It enjoyed an instant success, running through eleven editions in less than two years. The secret of the authorship was badly kept, and Gray presently became, in his thirty-fifth year, a celebrity as the 'maker of the Church-yard Essay.' He received, however, none of the profits, as, anticipating no success, he had presented the copyright to the publisher. Even in those days this was no slight gift; it was stated after the poet's death that Dodsley had made nearly a thousand pounds by the poetry of Gray, who himself realised by it forty pounds, not a penny more nor less, during the whole of his life.

There now follows another gap of two years in the record of the poet's career. We possess, for some unaccountable reason, no letters of his between the end of 1751 and the early part of 1753, except one brief note. He is once more called before us by the preparations made for the publication of his poems. As early as June 1751 Richard Bentley, the son of the famous Master of Trinity, was preparing, under Walpole's care, the illustrations for a luxurious collection of Gray's poems. They took a long time to finish, and the book did not see the light till March 1753, when it appeared in a thin folio form as *Designs by Mr. R. Bentley for Six Poems by Mr. T. Gray*. The six poems were the *Ode to Spring, Ode on Mr. Walpole's Cat*, the *Eton Ode, A Long Story, Hymn to Adversity*, and the *Elegy written* (no longer *wrote*) *in a Country Churchyard*. A few days after the publication of this volume, Gray's

mother died at Stoke, and was buried in the famous churchyard, where may still be read the epitaph which her son
composed for her tomb :—

In the same pious confidence, beside her sister and faithful friend,
sleep the remains of Dorothy Gray, widow, the careful tender mother
of many children, of whom one only had the misfortune to survive
her. She died March 11, 1753, aged 67 [1].

His surviving maternal aunt, Mrs. Rogers, now in her
seventy-eighth year, was joined at Stoke by his paternal
aunt, Mrs. Oliffe; after this Gray visited the house but
seldom, for he had an extreme dislike to Mrs. Oliffe, whom
he described as 'the Spawn of Cerberus upon the Dragon of
Wantley,' and, more roundly, as 'an old Harridan.' In the
autumn of 1753 he took the first of those journeys in search
of the picturesque in landscape and architecture, which now
became habitual with him in the long vacation. He was
writing very little verse; the only example which belongs to
these years is the fragmentary *Ode on Vicissitude*, which was
written early in 1754. To the same year belongs the interesting prose *Essay on Norman Architecture*, which was not
printed until 1814. Gray was the first modern student of
the history of architecture, and his notes on this subject are
so fresh and valuable that it is to be regretted that they are
so few.

At the close of 1754 Gray completed a very important
poem, an ode composed in competition with the triumphal
epinikia of Pindar. He circulated this in manuscript as an
'Ode in the Greek manner,' but it is known to us as *The
Progress of Poesy*. He was warned by his friends that he
would win no popularity by this austere species of writing,
but he answered 'that his taste for praise was not like that

---

[1] This is here printed from the original pencil note made by Gray
for the stonemason, who ventured in more than one instance slightly
to alter the wording.

of children for fruit; if there was nothing but medlars and blackberries in the world, he could be very well content to go without any at all'; he would have the best or none. Another Pindaric ode on *The Liberty of Genius* was planned about the same time, but of this there exists only a fragment of the argument. A third effort in the same direction, *The Bard*, although long delayed, was at length brought to a fortunate conclusion. The exordium of this poem, having occupied three months, was finished in March 1755, but it was exactly two years and five months in reaching completion, and the slowness of its growth was the subject of mirth with the poet himself, who called it 'Odikle,' and made fun of its stunted proportions.

In July of 1755 Gray made a tour in Hampshire, in the course of which he took a chill or else overtaxed his powers, with the result that for the rest of his life he was always more or less an invalid. Walpole was alarmed at the condition of his friend's health, and persuaded George Hervey, Earl of Bristol, who was named English Minister at Lisbon, to invite Gray to go with him to Portugal, then esteemed a sovereign retreat from illness of all sorts. The Minister made the offer, but Gray refused. In February 1756, one night, while he was asleep in his room at Peterhouse, a cruel practical joke was played upon him. He was induced, by shouts of 'fire,' to descend by a rope-ladder, which his extreme nervousness had caused him to provide, into a tub of water which the unmannerly undergraduates had placed under his window. He complained to the authorities, 'and not thinking that his remonstrance was sufficiently attended to, quitted the College.' He was received with open arms by his old friends at Pembroke, on the 6th of March, 1755, and there he resided till his death; comfortably lodged, surrounded by congenial friends, and, in his own words, 'as quiet as in the Grande Chartreuse.' He was the first, and for a long time the only person in the

University who made his rooms look pretty. He took care that his windows should be always full of mignonette or some other sweetly-scented plant, and he was famous for a pair of huge Japanese vases, in blue and white china. 'Removing myself,' he said, 'from Peterhouse to Pembroke may be looked upon as a sort of æra in a life so barren of events as mine.'

The Bard had long been laid aside, when a performance of the *Stabat Mater* of Pergolesi, and still more some concerts given at Cambridge by the blind harper, John Parry, induced Gray to resume and complete it in May 1757. He gave it, with *The Progress of Poesy*, to Horace Walpole, who made these poems the first issue of his printing-press at Strawberry Hill. On the 8th of August, 1757, appeared '*Odes* by Mr. Gray. Φωνᾶντα συνετοῖσι.' They enjoyed a great success among the discerning, to whom alone they were designed to be vocal. Goldsmith reviewed them, Garrick and Warburton eulogised them, Colman and Lloyd parodied them. Gray projected, in the same winter, a didactic poem on the Revival of Learning, but did not proceed with it. He was very feeble and distressed in health, and averse to action and society. At the death of Colley Cibber, in December 1757, the office of poet-laureate was offered to him, and refused. He said that he would 'rather be serjeant-trumpeter or pin-maker to the palace.' Whitehead (1715–1785) had fewer scruples, and accepted the office.

Gray was much engaged in private business in 1758, buying bric-à-brac and South Sea stock, and sinking a main portion of his property in an annuity, that he might enjoy a larger income. Mrs. Rogers died in September, and left Mrs. Oliffe joint executrix of her little property with Gray, who described himself as spending the month of November at Stoke 'agreeably employed in dividing nothing' with her. In January 1758 Mrs. Oliffe having taken herself off to Norfolk, Gray closed the little house at Stoke Poges, and from this time forth only visited the village, which had been his home for nearly twenty years, when he was invited to stay at Stoke House by Lady Cobham. At the same time, to the distress of his Cambridge friends, he ceased to reside in Pembroke, and spent the next three years in London.

He was among the throng of visitors who entered the British Museum when it was first thrown open to the public, on the 15th of January, 1759, and he had for some weeks past been living in Southampton Row, waiting for this event to take place. He was a daily frequenter of the Reading Room, then a mere basement chamber, 'with a wainscot table and twenty chairs.' He worked there at first for no literary or professional purpose, but because his principal pleasure was to steep himself in every species of learning. His lodgings, though now in the heart of London, were then pleasantly situated at the outskirts. His bedroom looked over a garden full of jessamine and roses, and his drawing-room over Bedford Gardens and a fine stretch of upland fields. He trudged down to Covent Garden every day in summer, for his sweet-peas and pinks, scarlet martagon-lilies, double stocks, and flowering marjoram. As he worked day by day at the Museum there grew up in him a desire to write a complete history of English Poetry. Pope had projected such a scheme, but on lines not nearly wide or scholarly enough. For this purpose Gray began to make copious transcriptions-from the Museum MSS. of Lydgate, Occleve, Wyatt, and others, and produced in these years a mass of rough material, which he afterwards presented to Thomas Warton (1728-1790) to aid him in his great enterprise.

Gray's life in London during these three years was exceedingly quiet and uneventful, broken only by rare visits to Dr. Wharton at Old Park, to Walpole at Strawberry Hill, and to Lady Cobham at Stoke. On the 23rd of September, 1759, the last-named friend, believing herself to be sinking, sent for Gray, and he was in very frequent attendance on her until April 1760, when she died. She left the whole of her property to her niece, Miss Harriet Speed, and there is reason to believe that she wished that the latter should marry Gray. He does not seem to have felt that he was a man whose age, health and spirits warranted his offering his hand to a young lady in the prime of life. Miss Speed preserved a warm affection for him, but eventually married a young Swiss nobleman much younger than herself, to Gray's sincere relief. During the winter of 1760 and the spring of 1761 Gray was giving his main attention to early English poetry. He worked at the British Museum with indefatigable zeal, copying with his own hand the whole of the very rare 1579 edition of Gawin Douglas' *Palace of Honour*, and composing his interesting and learned essays on *Metre* and on the *Poetry of John Lydgate*.

In the summer of 1761 his thoughts began to turn again to Cambridge, and he went back to his rooms in college. His life was now cheered by the companionship of a young undergraduate, afterwards known as the Rev. Norton Nicholls, of Blundeston, who made his acquaintance and became one of the most faithful of his friends. The personal reminiscences of Gray by Nicholls, not given to the world till 1843, present us with the most interesting and charming account of the poet's later years which we possess. Nothing could be more humdrum than Gray's existence after his return to Cambridge. There was no sign of literary life in him, and the only fact recorded about the year 1762 is that he took a journey through Yorkshire in the summer. On his return from this tour, however, he found his friends in a state of excitement. The Professor of Modern History and Languages at Cambridge, a nonentity named Shellet Turner, was dead, and Gray's friends thought that he ought to succeed him. He was persuaded to apply for the chair, but he met with a refusal. Six years later, when it again was vacant, it was offered to him, and accepted.

His study of Icelandic and interest in the northern literature of Europe dates from these years. His Eddaic poems *The Fatal Sisters* and *The Descent of Odin*, in which he developed a new romantic force of writing, were composed in 1761. Gray, it should be noted, takes precedence not only of Sir Walter Scott, Mr. Morris, and other British poets, but even of the countless Danish, Swedish, and German writers who for a century past have celebrated the adventures of the archaic heroes of their race. It is probable that he would have pushed further in this direction, if the condition of his health and spirits had not been such as to deprive him of all energy. During the winter of 1763 and spring of 1764 he suffered acutely, and at length had to undergo a dangerous operation. In July of the latter year this was successfully performed, and he was much relieved.

As soon as he could travel he went, as has lately been discovered, to Scotland, which he now visited for the first time. He got as far as Loch Lomond, and returned by Stirling and Edinburgh to his friends in the county of Durham. He then went south to Wiltshire and Hampshire, and returned to London after a holiday of some four months, much refreshed. The next year he went again to Scotland, as the guest of a Cambridge friend, Lord Strathmore, who took him for a tour in the Highlands and entertained him at his castle of Glamis. Gray was delighted; 'in short,' he says, 'since I saw the Alps, I have seen nothing sublime till now.' When he was at Glamis, the young poet James Beattie (1735-1803), afterwards author of *The Minstrel*, came from Aberdeen to visit him, and brought him an offer of the degree of Doctor of Laws from that university. Gray welcomed the visitor, but declined the honour. On his return from Scotland, he expressed his pleasure at the scenery in these terms:—

I am charmed with my expedition; it is of the Highlands I speak; the Lowlands are worth seeing once, but the mountains are ecstatic, and ought to be visited in pilgrimage once a year. None but these monstrous children of God know how to join so much beauty with so much horror. A fig for your poets, painters, gardeners, and clergymen, that have not been among them; their imagination can be made up of nothing but bowling-greens, flowering shrubs, horseponds, Fleet-ditches, shell-grottoes, and Chinese rails. Then I had so beautiful an autumn, Italy could hardly produce a nobler scene, and this so sweetly contrasted with that perfection of nastiness, and total want of accommodation, that Scotland can only supply.

Henceforth the chief events in Gray's life were his summer holidays. That of 1766 he passed in Kent, and wrote at Denton the powerful verses on Lord Holland's Villa. In 1767 he visited Dovedale and the Peak, and in September set off with Dr. Wharton to explore the Cumberland Lakes, but was forced, by his companion's illness, to return prematurely and almost without a glimpse of the mountains. In 1768 the first general edition of Gray's *Poems* was published by Dodsley, and more than 2000 copies were sold within four months. In the summer of the same year, Professor Brockett fell off his horse as he was riding homeward drunk, and broke his neck. Gray refused to lay himself open to a second rebuff, but the chair was given to him by the Duke of Grafton without his application. He delivered no lectures as Professor of Modern History and Modern Languages. It is, of course, unfortunate that he did not, but it should be remembered that there was nothing singular in this. Not one of his predecessors, from the date of the institution of the chair, had delivered a single lecture.

The Duke of Grafton succeeded the Duke of Newcastle as Chancellor of the University in 1768, and Gray volunteered to compose an ode to be performed at the ceremony of installation. This ode was given, with Dr. Randall's music, on the 1st of July, 1769, and was published by the University. This was the last of Gray's poems, and his career was nearing its term. He had, however, one more work to do, and that a considerable one. He was yet to discover and to describe the beauty of the Cambrian Lakes. In his youth he was the man who first looked on the sublimities of Alpine scenery with pleasure, and in old age he was to be the pioneer of Wordsworth in opening the eyes of Englishmen to the exquisite landscape of Cumberland. He started on this famous tour from Old Park, in the last days of September, 1769, and he returned to Cambridge late in October. The record of this excursion, the most delightful of Gray's prose-writings, was printed by Mason in 1775, and again, in a more accurate form, in 1884, by the present writer, who had access to the scattered portions of the poet's original manuscript.

In November, 1769, Norton Nicholls gave a note of introduction to Gray to a young Swiss gentleman, named Charles Victor de Bonstetten, who was proceeding to Cambridge to complete his education. Gray was instantly attracted to him, and found in his vivacity, ardour, and brightness an extraordinary charm. He secured Bonstetten a lodging close to Pembroke Hall, at a coffee-house, and set himself to superintend his studies. The attraction was mutual, and during the four months which the young Swiss spent in Cambridge, he was constantly in the company of the English poet. These strangely assorted friends spent every evening together, rejecting all other society, until the younger man had confided to the older all his hopes, experiences, and aspirations. Gray, on his part, confided nothing, but received Bonstetten's enthusiasm with the deepest interest and sympathy.

This final and most ardent friendship of Gray's life came too late; it disturbed and enfeebled him. When Bonstetten was called home in March 1770, the poet sank into complete dejection of spirits; 'Cambridge,' he said, 'never appeared so horrible to me as it does now.' After a while he buoyed himself up with the hope that when the summer came he would be able to visit Bonstetten in Switzerland, or at least in 1771, and after a miserable month or two he regained

something of his old serenity of spirits. He did not go to
Switzerland, but spent the summer instead in a tour with
Norton Nicholls through the midland counties and down the
Severn and the Wye. At Pembroke College, now that his
intimate friend James Brown was Master, Gray was practically allowed to do anything he liked, and he took the unusual step of lodging his aged aunt Mrs. Oliffe, now ninety
years of age, in college close to his own rooms, although
her asperity of temper was by no means assuaged. She died
there early in 1771.

All the preparations were made for a visit Gray and
Nicholls were to pay Bonstetten in the summer of that year,
but at the last moment the poet had to intimate that his
health was not equal to the exertion. Nicholls parted with
him in Gray's old rooms in Jermyn Street in June, and was
concerned and anxious to leave his friend so aged, dejected,
and invalided. On the 22nd of July, finding himself alone
in new lodgings he had taken in Kensington, and overwhelmed by a melancholy presentiment of death, Gray
suddenly returned to Cambridge. Two nights afterwards,
while dining in Pembroke College hall, close to the spot
where Mr. Thornycroft's marble bust of him was placed on
the 26th of May, 1885, he was suddenly attacked by nausea.
The gout which had so long been moving through his
system had now reached the stomach. He lingered until
Sunday, the 29th, when he was taken with a strong convulsive
fit, and these fits recurred until he died. After the last of them
he lay a long while in a stupor, supported in the arms of his
old friend, the Master, who had scarcely left him since the
first attack, and ceased to breathe an hour before midnight
on the 30th of July, 1771, in his fifty-fifth year. He was
buried, as his will directed, by the side of his mother, in the
churchyard of Stoke Poges.

Gray was a little fair man, of fastidious habits and dainty
appearance. He was very chilly and reserved in his address

to strangers, and very shy of forming new acquaintances ; during the last years of his life at Cambridge, it was very difficult even to get a sight of him. He protected himself against impertinence by an air of great affectation, which annoyed his friends, who did not wish the world to suppose this very sincere and estimable man to be supercilious or effeminate. He was exceedingly suppressed and noiseless in manner, but constantly at work. Activity was his great protection against constitutional melancholy ; 'to be employed,' he used to say, 'is to be happy.'

His acquirements, the result of a life spent in this unceasing scholastic industry, were unique. He knew, it may roughly be said, whatever there was to be known in his age. One of those best qualified to judge pronounced him 'perhaps the most learned man in Europe : he was fully acquainted with the elegant and profound parts of science, and not superficially but thoroughly. He knew every branch of history, both natural and civil; had read all the original historians of England, France, and Italy; and was a great antiquary. Criticism, metaphysics, morals, politics, made a principal part of his plan of study. Voyages and travels of all sorts were his principal amusement; and he had a fine taste in painting, prints, architecture, and gardening.'. In his letters, which are among the most entertaining in the language, the results of all this comprehensive acquirement are highly apparent, but are kept in the background by his humour, which bubbles and flashes everywhere, and by his great natural warmth of affection. He was never married ; but the absence of this tie seemed only to serve to quicken his sense of the duty he owed as a son, as a relative, and as a friend. In the latter capacity he is pre-eminent among men of letters. Judged merely as an author, it may be said without injustice, that he is the only amateur that has ever succeeded in winning a place abreast of the great professional writers of this nation.

The verse of Gray is smaller in bulk than that of any other considerable English poet, but its quality is of a very high order. Poetry may be either spontaneous or deliberate; it may be thrown down the mountain-side in a cascade, or drawn along the valley in conduits. Of the former class Burns is the type in our language; Gray is certainly the type of the latter. The late Mr. Mark Pattison has given the first place in English literature to Gray as an artist in verse. 'As a *poet*,' he says, 'Pope is surpassed by many in our language; as a literary artist, by Gray alone.' The language of Adam Smith and of Sir James Mackintosh was almost identical with this; and in our own time Mr. Matthew Arnold, surveying with his wonted serenity the whole body of English poetry, has endorsed their praise with very little abatement. It may therefore be easily understood that though far from being the most moving or the most inspired of English poets, Gray is the one from whom the young student can learn most about the art and business of poetry. In reading him, he can 'feel the very pulse of the machine,' and be taught as a pupil of painting or sculpture is taught, by standing behind the master's hand while it is actually at work. Gray's verse is not faultless, but it is as difficult to find flaws in it, as to find them in any poet's writing over which a century of criticism has passed. It is certainly not merely the best verse, but the best poetry also, between the heyday of the classical school and the complete romantic revival. Gray has, at least, no rival between Pope and Cowper.

When he was a boy and beginning to take an intelligent interest in poetry, the English classical school had reached its meridian and had begun to decline. The stiff manner of composing verses, which Waller (1605-1687) had invented nearly a century before, had reached its meridian, and was visibly declining. By the time that Gray was fourteen, Southerne was the only survivor among the great dramatists of the Restoration. Pope (1688-1744) was the principal figure of the day. He had just published the *Dunciad*, he was writing the *Essay on Man*, he was the most distinguished literary figure alive in Europe. But the friends and foes that had surrounded him were dispersing. Addison, Steele, Prior, Parnell, and Garth were dead, and Gay was dying. Pope himself, the central luminary, was shining as brilliantly as ever, but all the rest were fading. The last powers of Swift were being expended on political lampoons; Tickell, Arbuthnot and Mandeville were to be silent for the future. Since the early manhood of Pope few new poets had arisen, except his more or less ephemeral imitators. The most prominent names in 1730 were these:—Edward Young (1684-1765), now approaching middle life, and presently to become famous as the author of *Night Thoughts*; James Thomson (1700-1748), the leading poet among the younger men in England, just coming into repute through successive instalments of his *Seasons*; John Dyer (1699-1758), a pensive descriptive writer, whose *Grongar Hill* was a feeble attempt at a return to the romantic manner; and Matthew Green (1696-1737), whose humoristic and picturesque studies, of extraordinary felicity in the Dutch order, were only known as yet to his private friends. Somerville, Blair, Glover and Armstrong, like Green, had as yet published little or nothing.

Thomson was, in short, the only young poet in England who was proving to the world that he possessed any literary vitality. How this general sterility, which in a few years became, if possible, even more universal, would affect a mind like Gray's, Mr. Matthew Arnold has stated with great clearness. 'Gray,' he says, 'a born poet, fell upon an age of prose. He fell upon an age whose task was such as to call forth, in general, men's powers of understanding, wit and cleverness, rather than their deepest powers of mind and soul. As regards literary production, the task of the eighteenth century in England was not the poetic interpretation of the world, its task was to create a plain, clear, straightforward, efficient prose. Poetry obeyed the bent of mind requisite for the due fulfilment of this task of the century. It was intellectual, argumentative, ingenious; not seeing things in their truth and beauty, not interpretative. Gray, with the qualities of mind and soul of a genuine poet, was isolated in his century, maintaining and fortifying them by lofty studies, he yet could not fully educe and enjoy them; the want of a genial atmosphere, the failure of sympathy in his contemporaries, were too great.'

Against this 'spiritual east wind,' Gray found his protection by sheltering himself behind the great writers of the preceding century. Unfortunately, in some respects, for his style, he did not seek that shelter far enough back; he was too easily content with Cowley and Dryden, and did not become a student of Shakespeare and the contemporaries of Shakespeare until his ear was formed. The men of the Restoration, however, had something to give him which their followers had lost. Pope, with his brilliant art, was a less generous versifier for a youth to imitate than Cowley with his occasional bursts of noble music, than Dryden with his

Coursers of ethereal race,
With necks in thunder cloth'd, and long-resounding pace.

These fathers of the classical school still had echoes of an earlier time in their voices, and Gray's memory was indelibly impressed with them. He told Beattie, long afterwards, that 'if there was any excellence in his own numbers, he had learned it wholly from that great poet,' Dryden. This was an exaggeration, and the remark is doubtless incorrectly reported, but he had learned much. His debt to Cowley is not less surely acknowledged by the reminiscences of that writer which are found in Gray's early odes. He had, however, other masters than these. He learned much from Milton, whose sublimity of language and whose transcendental order of imagination had great attractions for him; from Green and Gresset (1709-1777), those elegant Dutch artists in English and French octosyllabics; but most of all from the Greek poets, who taught him to subdue his melody and grandeur, his delicacy and wit, to the laws of harmony and of a correct and sustained evolution.

The term 'evolution,' as applied in poetical criticism, describes the mode in which a poem is built up, or grows up, like a building or a tree, into the certain form which is the most appropriate and sufficient for the thoughts and images which possess the poet's mind. Much admirable poetry, most poetry of the romantic class, has no evolution at all, but ceases abruptly, when the emotion flags. It is a mark of the artist, as opposed to the improvisatore, to be solicitous about this matter, and no one was ever more solicitous than Gray. An ode of Cowley's, or even of Collins's or Shelley's, is apt to be a cluster of stanzas loosely joined together, and more or less beautiful in the detail of its parts. The least inspired of Gray's odes has this peculiarity, that it starts from a point which the poet has fixed upon, covers a certain area of thought which he has accurately measured, and closes inevitably at the moment when he has said all that occurs to him, and no more.

It should be here admitted that this serenity of execution, this command of the poet's art, do not strike all capable critics as praiseworthy. Coleridge found the skill of Gray mechanical, and in our own day Mr. Swinburne has complained of 'the fanfaronade and falsetto which impair the always rhetorically elaborate and sometimes genuinely sonorous notes of Gray.' It must be admitted that the style of Gray, especially in his early writings, is marred by the faults of his age, a tendency to excessive use of allegory, a foible for being brilliant rather than genuine and tender. On the whole, however, it must be confessed that he seldom wanders far from the path he laid before him; his own words are, 'the style I have aimed at is extreme conciseness of expression, yet pure, perspicuous and musical.' His own contemporaries complained that he was not perspicuous, but this was inattention on their part.

His poetry may be roughly divided into two great sections, his rhetorical and his romantic pieces. His odes are of two orders, but both belong to the rhetorical section. In his earlier odes he may be vaguely called Horatian, in his later ones more distinctly Pindaric. In both he keeps close to the traditions of the history of poetry, at first without straying very far even from the diction of his predecessors. The romantic section of his work includes the famous and unrivalled *Elegy*, and the various small lyrics which he composed, on foreign themes, after his imagination had become stirred by Ossian, Percy, and the Edda. The *Elegy*, in spite of the fact that its inspiration flags towards the close, is one of the most surprising productions of English poetry, and the most deservedly popular single piece in our literature. Encrusted as it is with layers upon layers of eulogy, bibliography and criticism, we have but to scrape these away to find the immortal poem beneath as fresh, as melodious, as inspiring as ever. The student should strive to repeat to himself its hackneyed and proverbial lines as though he had never met with them before, and assure himself, as though the poem were still unknown, of their extraordinary felicity. He will return to the other poems of Gray with a consciousness that, in spite of all his art and splendour as a lyrist, it is 'as an elegiac poet that Gray holds for all ages to come his unassailable and sovereign station.'

POEMS.

POEMS.

ODE TO THE SPRING.

Lo! where the rosy-bosom'd Hours,
    Fair Venus' train appear,
Disclose the long-expecting flowers,
    And wake the purple year!
The Attic warbler pours her throat   5
Responsive to the cuckow's note,
    The untaught harmony of spring:
While whisp'ring pleasure as they fly,
Cool Zephyrs thro' the clear blue sky
    Their gather'd fragrance fling.   10

Where'er the oak's thick branches stretch
    A broader browner shade;
Where'er the rude and moss-grown beech
    O'er-canopies the glade,
Beside some water's rushy brink   15
With me the Muse shall sit, and think
    (At ease reclin'd in rustic state)
How vain the ardour of the Crowd,
How low, how little are the Proud,
    How indigent the Great!   20

ODE ON THE SPRING.

Still is the toiling hand of Care:
The panting herds repose:
Yet hark, how thro' the peopled air
The busy murmur glows:
The insect youth are on the wing, 25
Eager to taste the honied spring,
 And float amid the liquid noon:
Some lightly o'er the current skim,
Some shew their gayly-gilded trim
 Quick-glancing to the sun. 30

To Contemplation's sober eye
Such is the race of Man:
And they that creep, and they that fly,
 Shall end where they began.
Alike the Busy and the Gay 35
But flutter thro' life's little day,
 In fortune's varying colours drest:
Brush'd by the hand of rough Mischance,
Or chill'd by age, their airy dance
 They leave, in dust to rest. 40

Methinks I hear in accents low
The sportive kind reply:
Poor moralist! and what art thou?
 A solitary fly!
Thy Joys no glittering female meets, 45
No hive hast thou of hoarded sweets,
 No painted plumage to display:
On hasty wings thy youth is flown;
Thy sun is set, thy spring is gone—
 We frolick, while 'tis May. 50

ODE ON THE DEATH OF A FAVOURITE CAT,

DROWNED IN A TUB OF GOLD FISHES.

'TWAS on a lofty vase's side,
Where China's gayest art had dy'd
   The azure flowers, that blow;
Demurest of the tabby kind,
The pensive Selima reclin'd,   5
   Gazed on the lake below.

Her conscious tail her joy declar'd;
The fair round face, the snowy beard,
   The velvet of her paws,
Her coat, that with the tortoise vies,   10
Her ears of jet, and emerald eyes,
   She saw; and purr'd applause.

Still had she gaz'd; but 'midst the tide
Two angel forms were seen to glide,
   The Genii of the stream: 15
Their scaly armour's Tyrian hue
Thro' richest purple to the view
   Betray'd a golden gleam.

The hapless Nymph with wonder saw:
A whisker first and then a claw,   20
   With many an ardent wish,
She stretch'd in vain to reach the prize.
What female heart can gold despise?
   What Cat's averse to fish?

32   ODE ON A DISTANT PROSPECT

Presumptuous Maid ! with looks intent   25
Again she stretch'd, again she bent,
  Nor knew the gulf between.
(Malignant Fate sat by, and smil'd)
The slipp'ry verge her feet beguil'd,
  She tumbled headlong in.   30

Eight times emerging from the flood
She mew'd to ev'ry watry God,
  Some speedy aid to send.
No Dolphin came, no Nereid stirr'd:
Nor cruel *Tom*, nor *Susan* heard.   35
  A Fav'rite has no friend!

From hence, ye Beauties, undeceiv'd,
Know, one false step is ne'er retriev'd,
  And be with caution bold.
Not all that tempts your wand'ring eyes   40
And heedless hearts, is lawful prize ;
  'Nor all, that glisters, gold.

ODE ON A DISTANT PROSPECT OF ETON COLLEGE.

Ye distant spires, ye antique towers,
  That crown the watry glade,
Where grateful Science still adores
  Her HENRY'S holy Shade ;
And ye, that from the stately brow   5
Of WINDSOR'S heights th' expanse below

OF ETON COLLEGE. 33

Of grove, of lawn, of mead survey,
Whose turf, whose shade, whose flowers among
Wanders the hoary Thames along
 —His silver-winding way: 10

Ah, happy hills, ah, pleasing shade,
 Ah, fields belov'd in vain,
Where once my careless childhood stray'd,
 A stranger yet to pain!
I feel the gales, that from ye blow, 15
 A momentary bliss bestow,
As waving fresh their gladsome wing,
My weary soul they seem to sooth,
And, redolent of joy and youth,
 To breathe a second spring.   20

Say, father THAMES, for thou hast seen
 Full many a sprightly race
Disporting on thy margent green
 The paths of pleasure trace,
Who foremost now delight to cleave 25
With pliant arm thy glassy wave?
The captive linnet which enthrall?
What idle progèny succeed
To chase the rolling circle's speed,
 Or urge the flying ball?   30

While some on earnest business bent
 Their murm'ring labours ply
'Gainst graver hours, that bring constraint
 To sweeten liberty:
Some bold adventurers disdain 35
The limits of their little reign,

D

And unknown regions dare descry:
Still as they run they look behind,
They hear a voice in every wind,
And snatch a fearful joy. (40)

Gay hope is theirs by fancy fed,
Less pleasing when possest ;
The tear forgot as soon as shed,
The sunshine of the breast :
Theirs buxom health of rosy hue, 45
Wild wit, invention ever-new,
And lively chear of vigour born ;
The thoughtless day, the easy night,
The spirits pure, the slumbers light,
That fly th' approach of morn. 50

Alas, regardless of their doom
The little victims play !
No sense have they of ills to come,
Nor care beyond to-day :
Yet see how all around 'em wait 55
The Ministers of human fate,
And black Misfortune's baleful train !
Ah, shew them where in ambush stand
To seize their prey the murth'rous band !
Ah, tell them, they are men ! 60

These shall the fury Passions tear,
The vulturs of the mind,
Disdainful Anger, pallid Fear,
And Shame that sculks behind ;
Or pineing Love shall waste their youth, 65
Or Jealousy with rankling tooth,

That inly gnaws the secret heart,
And Envy wan, and faded Care,
Grim-visag'd comfortless Despair,
  And Sorrow's piercing dart.

Ambition this shall tempt to rise,
Then whirl the wretch from high,
To bitter Scorn a sacrifice,
  And grinning Infamy.
The stings of Falshood those shall try,.
And hard Unkindness' alter'd eye,
  That mocks the tear it forc'd to flow;
And keen Remorse with blood defil'd,
And moody Madness laughing wild
  Amid severest woe.

Lo, in the vale of years beneath
A griesly troop are seen,
The painful family of Death,
  More hideous than their Queen:
This racks the joints, this fires the veins,
That every labouring sinew strains,
  Those in the deeper vitals rage:
Lo, Poverty, to fill the band,
That numbs the soul with icy hand,
  And slow-consuming Age.

To each his suff'rings: all are men,
  Condemn'd alike to groan,
The tender for another's pain;
  Th' unfeeling for his own.
Yet, ah! why should they know their fate?
Since sorrow never comes too late,

And happiness too swiftly flies,
Thought would destroy their paradise.
No more ; where ignorance is bliss,
'Tis folly to be wise.   100

HYMN TO ADVERSITY.

DAUGHTER of Jove, relentless Power,
   Thou Tamer of the human breast,
Whose iron scourge and tort'ring hour
   The Bad affright, afflict the Best!
Bound in thy adamantine chain,   5
The Proud are taught to taste of pain,
And purple Tyrants vainly groan
With pangs unfelt before, unpitied and alone.

When first thy Sire to send on earth,
   Virtue, his darling Child, design'd,   10
To thee he gave the heav'nly Birth,
   And bad to form her infant mind.
Stern rugged Nurse! thy rigid lore
With patience many a year she bore :
What sorrow was, thou bad'st her know,   15
And from her own she learn'd to melt at others' woe.

Scared at thy frown terrific, fly
   Self-pleasing Folly's idle brood,
Wild Laughter, Noise, and thoughtless Joy,
   And leave us leisure to be good.   20

HYMN TO ADVERSITY.

Light they disperse, and with them go
The summer Friend, the flatt'ring Foe;
By vain Prosperity received,
To her they vow their truth, and are again believed.

Wisdom in sable garb array'd   25
   Immers'd in rapt'rous thought profound,
And Melancholy, silent maid,
   With leaden eye, that loves the ground,
Still on thy solemn steps attend :
Warm Charity, the gen'ral Friend,   30
   With Justice to herself severe,
And Pity, dropping soft the sadly-pleasing tear.

Oh, gently on thy Suppliant's head,
   Dread goddess, lay thy chast'ning hand!
Not in thy Gorgon terrors clad,   35
   Not circled with the vengeful Band
(As by the Impious thou art seen)
With thund'ring voice, and threat'ning mien,
   With screaming Horror's funeral cry,
Despair, and fell Disease, and ghastly Poverty.

Thy form benign,- oh Goddess, wear,
   Thy milder influence impart,
Thy philosophic Train be there
   To soften, not to wound my heart.
The gen'rous spark extinct revive,   45
Teach me to love and to forgive,
   Exact my own defects to scan,
What others are, to feel, and know myself a Man.

THE PROGRESS OF POESY.

A PINDARIC ODE.

I. 1.

AWAKE, Æolian lyre, awake,
And give to rapture all thy trembling strings.
From Helicon's harmonious springs
A thousand rills their mazy progress take:
The laughing flowers, that round them blow,   5
Drink life and fragrance as they flow.
Now the rich stream of music winds along
Deep, majestic, smooth, and strong.
Thro' verdant vales, and Ceres' golden reign:
Now rowling down the steep amain,   10
Headlong, impetuous, see it pour;
The rocks and nodding groves rebellow to the roar.

I. 2.

Oh! Sovereign of the willing soul,
Parent of sweet and solemn-breathing airs,
Enchanting shell! the sullen Cares   15
And frantic Passions hear thy soft controul.
On Thracia's hills the Lord of War
Has curb'd the fury of his car,
And drop'd his thirsty lance at thy command.
Perching on the scept'red hand   20
Of Jove, thy magic lulls the feather'd king
With ruffled plumes, and flagging wing:
Quench'd in dark clouds of slumber lie
The terror of his beak, and light'nings of his eye.

I. 3.

Thee the voice, the dance, obey, 25
Temper'd to thy warbled lay.
O'er Idalia's velvet-green
The rosy-crowned Loves are seen
On Cytherea's day.
With antic Sports, and blue-eyed Pleasures, 30
Frisking light in frolic measures;
Now pursuing, now retreating,
   Now in circling troops they meet:
To brisk notes in cadence beating,
   Glance their many-twinkling feet. 35
Slow melting strains their Queen's approach declare:
   Where'er she turns the Graces homage pay.
With arms sublime, that float upon the air,
   In gliding state she wins her easy way:
O'er her warm cheek, and rising bosom, move 40
The bloom of young Desire, and purple light of Love.

II. 1.

   Man's feeble race what Ills await,
Labour, and Penury, the racks of Pain,
Disease, and Sorrow's weeping train,
   And Death, sad refuge from the storms of Fate! 45
The fond complaint, my Song, disprove,
And justify the laws of Jove.
Say, has he giv'n in vain the heav'nly Muse?
Night, and all her sickly dews,
Her Spectres wan, and Birds of boding cry, 50
He gives to range the dreary sky:
Till down the eastern cliffs afar
Hyperion's march they spy, and glitt'ring shafts of war.

II. 2.

In climes beyond the solar road,
Where shaggy forms o'er ice-built mountains roam, 55
The Muse has broke the twilight-gloom
To chear the shiv'ring Native's dull abode.
And oft, beneath the od'rous shade
Of Chili's boundless forests laid,
She deigns to hear the savage Youth repeat 60
In loose numbers wildly sweet
Their feather-cinctur'd Chiefs, and dusky Loves.
Her track, where'er the Goddess roves,
Glory pursue, and generous Shame,
Th' unconquerable Mind, and Freedom's holy flame. 65

II. 3.

Woods, that wave o'er Delphi's steep,
Isles, that crown th' Egæan deep,
Fields, that cool Ilissus laves,
Or where Mæander's amber waves
In lingering Lab'rinths creep, 70
How do your tuneful Echo's languish,
Mute, but to the voice of Anguish?
Where each old poetic Mountain
Inspiration breath'd around:
Ev'ry shade and hallow'd Fountain 75
Murmur'd deep a solemn sound: .
Till the sad Nine in Greece's evil hour,
Left their Parnassus for the Latian plains.
Alike they scorn the pomp of tyrant-Power,
And coward Vice, that revels in her chains. 80
When Latium had her lofty spirit lost,
They sought, oh Albion! next thy sea-encircled coast.

III. 1.

Far from the sun and summer-gale,
In thy green lap was Nature's Darling laid,
What time, where lucid Avon stray'd,   85
To Him the mighty Mother did unveil
Her aweful face : The dauntless Child
Stretch'd forth his little arms, and smiled.
This pencil take (she said), whose colours clear
Richly paint the vernal year :   90
Thine too these golden keys, immortal Boy!
This can unlock the gates of Joy ;
Of Horrour that, and thrilling Fears,
Or ope the sacred source of sympathetic Tears.

III. 2.

Nor second He, that rode sublime   95
Upon the seraph-wings of Extasy,
The secrets of th' Abyss to spy.
He pass'd the flaming bounds of Place and Time :
The living Throne, the saphire-blaze,
Where Angels tremble, while they gaze,   100
He saw ; but blasted with excess of light,
Closed his eyes in endless night.
Behold, where Dryden's less presumptuous car,
Wide o'er the fields of Glory bear
Two Coursers of ethereal race,   105
With necks in thunder cloath'd, and long-resounding pace.

III. 3.

Hark, his hands the lyre explore!
Bright-eyed Fancy hovering o'er .
Scatters from her pictur'd urn
Thoughts, that breath, and words, that burn.   110

But ah! 'tis heard no more——
Oh! Lyre divine, what daring Spirit
Wakes thee now? tho' he inherit
Nor the pride, nor ample pinion,
That the Theban Eagle bear   115
Sailing with supreme dominion
  Thro' the azure deep of air:
Yet oft before his infant eyes would run
  Such forms, as glitter in the Muse's ray,
With orient hues, unborrow'd of the Sun: 120
  Yet shall he mount, and keep his distant way
Beyond the limits of a vulgar fate,
Beneath the Good how far—but far above the Great.

THE BARD.

A PINDARIC ODE.

I. 1.

'RUIN seize thee, ruthless King!
Confusion on thy banners wait,
Tho' fann'd by Conquest's crimson wing
  They mock the air with idle state.
Helm, nor Hauberk's twisted mail,   5
Nor even thy virtues, Tyrant, shall avail
  To save thy secret soul from nightly fears,
  From Cambria's curse, from Cambria's tears!'
Such were the sounds, that o'er the crested pride
  Of the first Edward scatter'd wild dismay,   10

THE BARD. 43

As down the steep of Snowdon's shaggy side
　He wound with toilsome march his long array.
Stout Glo'ster stood aghast in speechless trance :
—To arms ! cried Mortimer, and couch'd his quiv'ring lance.

I. 2.

On a rock, whose haughty brow　　　　　　　　15
Frowns o'er old Conway's foaming flood,
　Robed in the sable garb of woe,
With haggard eyes the Poet stood ;
(Loose his beard, and hoary hair
Stream'd, like a meteor, to the troubled air)　　20
And with a Master's hand, and Prophet's fire,
Struck the deep sorrows of his lyre.
　' Hark, how each giant-oak, and desert cave,
Sighs to the torrent's aweful voice beneath !
O'er thee, oh King ! their hundred arms they wave,　25
　Revenge on thee in hoarser murmurs breath ;
Vocal no more, since Cambria's fatal day,
To high-born Hoel's harp, or soft Llewellyn's lay.'

I. 3.

　' Cold is Cadwallo's tongue,
That hush'd the stormy main :　　　　　　　　30
Brave Urien sleeps upon his craggy bed :
　Mountains, ye mourn in vain
　Modred, whose magic song
Made huge Plinlimmon bow his cloud-top'd head.
　On dreary Arvon's shore they lie,　　　　　　35
Smear'd with gore, and ghastly pale :
Far, far aloof th' affrighted ravens sail ;
　The famish'd Eagle screams, and passes by.

THE BARD.

Dear lost companions of my tuneful art,
  Dear, as the light that visits these sad eyes,   40
Dear, as the ruddy drops that warm my heart,
  Ye died amidst your dying country's cries—
No more I weep. They do not sleep.
  On yonder cliffs, a griesly band,
I see them sit, they linger yet,   45
  Avengers of their native land:
With me in dreadful harmony they join,
And weave with bloody hands the tissue of thy line.'

II. 1.

'Weave the warp, and weave the woof,
The winding-sheet of Edward's race.   50
  Give ample room, and verge enough
The characters of hell to trace.
Mark the year, and mark the night,
When Severn shall re-eccho with affright
The shrieks of death, thro' Berkley's roofs that ring,   55
Shrieks of an agonizing King!
  She-Wolf of France, with unrelenting fangs,
That tear'st the bowels of thy mangled Mate,
  From thee be born, who o'er thy country hangs
The scourge of Heav'n. What Terrors round him wait!   60
Amazement in his van, with Flight combined,
And sorrow's faded form, and solitude behind.'

II. 2.

'Mighty Victor, mighty Lord!
Low on his funeral couch he lies!
  No pitying heart, no eye, afford   65
A tear to grace his obsequies.

Is the sable Warriour fled?
Thy son is gone. He rests among the Dead.
The Swarm, that in thy noon-tide beam were born?
Gone to salute the rising Morn. 70
Fair laughs the Morn, and soft the Zephyr blows,
  While proudly riding o'er the azure realm
In gallant trim the gilded Vessel goes;
  Youth on the prow, and Pleasure at the helm;
Regardless of the sweeping Whirlwind's sway, 75
That, hush'd in grim repose, expects his evening-prey.'

II. 3.

'Fill high the sparkling bowl,
  The rich repast prepare,
  Reft of a crown, he yet may share the feast:
Close by the regal chair 80
  Fell Thirst and Famine scowl
  A baleful smile upon their baffled Guest.
Heard ye the din of battle bray,
  Lance to lance, and horse to horse?
  Long Years of havock urge their destined course, 85
And thro' the kindred squadrons mow their way.
  Ye Towers of Julius, London's lasting shame,
With many a foul and midnight murther fed,
  Revere his Consort's faith, his Father's fame,
And spare the meek Usurper's holy head. 90
Above, below, the rose of snow,
  Twined with her blushing foe, we spread:
The bristled Boar in infant-gore
  Wallows beneath the thorny shade.
Now, Brothers, bending o'er th' accursed loom 95
Stamp we our vengeance deep, and ratify his doom.'

III. 1.

'Edward, lo! to sudden fate
(Weave we the woof. The thread is spun.)
Half of thy heart we consecrate.
(The web is wove. The work is done.)   100
Stay, oh stay! nor thus forlorn
Leave me unbless'd, unpitied, here to mourn:
In yon bright track, that fires the western skies,
They melt, they vanish from my eyes,
But oh! what solemn scenes on Snowdon's height   105
    Descending slow their glitt'ring skirts unroll?
Visions of glory, spare my aching sight,
    Ye unborn Ages, crowd not on my soul!
No more our long-lost Arthur we bewail.
All hail, ye genuine Kings, Britannia's Issue, hail!'   110

III. 2.

'Girt with many a Baron bold
Sublime their starry fronts they rear;
    And gorgeous Dames, and Statesmen old
In bearded majesty, appear,
In the midst a Form divine!   115
Her eye proclaims her of the Briton-Line;
Her lyon-port, her awe-commanding face,
Attemper'd sweet to virgin-grace.
What strings symphonious tremble in the air,
    What strains of vocal transport round her play!   120
Hear from the grave, great Taliessin, hear;
    They breathe a soul to animate thy clay.
Bright Rapture calls, and soaring, as she sings,
Waves in the eye of Heav'n her many-colour'd wings.'

III. 3.

'The verse adorn again 125
   Fierce War, and faithful Love,
And Truth severe, by fairy Fiction drest.
   In buskin'd measures move
Pale Grief, and pleasing Pain,
With Horrour, Tyrant of the throbbing breast. 130
   A Voice, as of the Cherub-Choir,
Gales from blooming Eden bear;
And distant warblings lessen on my ear,
   That lost in long futurity expire.
Fond impious Man, think'st thou, yon sanguine cloud, 135
   Rais'd by thy breath, has quench'd the Orb of day?
To-morrow he repairs the golden flood,
   And warms the nations with redoubled ray.
Enough for me: With joy I see
   The different doom our Fates assign. 140
Be thine Despair, and scept'red Care,
   To triumph, and to die, are mine.'
He spoke, and headlong from the mountain's height
Deep in the roaring tide he plung'd to endless night.

THE FATAL SISTERS.

ADVERTISEMENT.

The Author once had thoughts (in concert with a Friend) of giving *the History of English Poetry:* In the Introduction to it he meant to have produced some specimens of the Style that reigned in ancient times among the neighbouring nations, or those who had subdued the greater part of this Island, and were our Progenitors: the following three Imitations made a part of them. He has long since drop'd his design, especially after he heard, that it was already in the hands of a Person [1] well qualified to do it justice, both by his taste, and his researches into antiquity.—[Gray.]

THE FATAL SISTERS.

AN ODE.

PREFACE.—In the Eleventh Century, *Sigurd*, Earl of the Orkney-Islands, went with a fleet of ships and a considerable body of troops into Ireland, to the assistance of *Sictryg with the silken beard*, who was then making war on his father-in-law *Brian*, King of Dublin: the Earl and all his forces were cut to pieces, and *Sictryg* was in danger of a total defeat; but the enemy had a greater loss by the death of *Brian* their King, who fell in the action. On Christmas Day (the day of the battle), a Native of *Caithness* in Scotland saw at a distance a number of persons on horseback riding full speed towards a hill, and seeming to enter into it. Curiosity led him to follow them, till looking through an opening in the rocks, he saw twelve gigantic figures resembling women; they were all employed about a loom; and as they wove, they sung the following dreadful Song; which, when they had finished, they tore the web into twelve pieces, and (each taking her portion) galloped Six to the North, and as many to the South.—[Gray, 1768.]

\ Now the storm begins to lower
(Haste, the loom of Hell prepare,)
Iron-sleet of arrowy shower
Hurtles in the darken'd air.

[1] Thomas Warton, the poet-laureate.—[ED.]

THE FATAL SISTERS.

Glitt'ring lances are the loom;
    Where the dusky warp we strain,
Weaving many a Soldier's doom,
    Orkney's woe, and Randver's bane.

See the griesly texture grow!
    ('Tis of human entrails made)
And the weights, that play below,
    Each a gasping Warriour's head.

Shafts for shuttles, dipt in gore,
    Shoot the trembling cords along.
Sword, that once a Monarch bore,
    Keep the tissue close and strong.

Mista black, terrific Maid,
    Sangrida, and Hilda see,
Join the wayward work to aid:
    Tis the woof of victory.

Ere the ruddy sun be set,
    Pikes must shiver, javelins sing,
Blade with clattering buckler meet,
    Hauberk crash, and helmet ring.

(Weave the crimson web of war)
    Let us go, and let us fly,
Where our Friends the conflict share,
    Where they triumph, where they die.

As the paths of fate we tread,
    Wading through th' ensanguin'd field,
Gondula, and Geira, spread
    O'er the youthful King your shield.

THE FATAL SISTERS.

We the reins to slaughter give,
  Ours to kill, and ours to spare :
Spite of danger he shall live.   35
  (Weave the crimson web of war.)

They, whom once the desart-beach
  Pent within its bleak domain,
Soon their ample sway shall stretch
  O'er the plenty of the plain.   40

Low the dauntless Earl is laid,
  Gor'd with many a gaping wound :
Fate demands a nobler head ;
  Soon a King shall bite the ground.

Long his loss shall Eirin weep,   45
  Ne'er again his likeness see ;
Long her strains in sorrow steep :
  Strains of Immortality !

Horror covers all the heath,
  Clouds of carnage blot the sun.   50
Sisters, weave the web of death ;
  Sisters, cease, the work is done.

Hail the task, and hail the hands !
  Songs of joy and triumph sing !
Joy to the victorious bands ;   55
  Triumph to the younger King.

Mortal, thou that hear'st the tale,
  Learn the tenour of our song.
Scotland, thro' each winding vale
  Far and wide the notes prolong.   60

Sisters, hence with spurs of speed :
Each her thundering faulchion wield ;
Each bestride her sable steed.
Hurry, hurry to the field.

THE DESCENT OF ODIN.

UPROSE the King of Men with speed,
And saddled strait his coal-black steed ;
Down the yawning steep he rode,
That leads to HELA'S drear abode.
Him the Dog of Darkness spied,   5
His shaggy throat he open'd wide,
While from his jaws, with carnage fill'd,
Foam and human gore distill'd :
Hoarse he bays with hideous din,
Eyes that glow, and fangs that grin ;   10
And long pursues, with fruitless yell,
The Father of the powerful spell.
Onward still his way he takes
(The groaning earth beneath him shakes,)
Till full before his fearless eyes   •   15
The portals nine of hell arise.
 Right against the eastern gate,
By the moss-grown pile he sate ;
Where long of yore to sleep was laid
The dust of the prophetic Maid.   20
Facing to the northern clime,
Thrice he traced the runic rhyme ;

THE DESCENT OF ODIN.

Thrice pronounc'd, in accents dread,
The thrilling verse that wakes the Dead:
Till from out the hollow ground   25
Slowly breath'd a sullen sound.

Pr. What call unknown, what charms presume
To break the quiet of the tomb?
Who thus afflicts my troubled sprite,
And drags me from the realms of night?   30
Long on these mould'ring bones have beat
The winter's snow, the summer's heat,
The drenching dews, and driving rain!
Let me, let me sleep again.
Who is he, with voice unblest,   35
That calls me from the bed of rest?

O. A Traveller, to thee unknown,
Is he that calls, a Warriour's Son.
Thou the deeds of light shalt know;
Tell me what is done below,   40
For whom yon glitt'ring board is spread,
Drest for whom yon golden bed.

Pr. Mantling in the goblet see
The pure bev'rage of the bee,
O'er it hangs the shield of gold;   45
'Tis the drink of Balder bold:
Balder's head to death is giv'n.
Pain can reach the Sons of Heav'n!
Unwilling I my lips unclose:
Leave me, leave me to repose.   50

O. Once again my call obey,
Prophetess, arise, and say,

THE DESCENT OF ODIN.

What dangers Odin's Child await,
Who the Author of his fate.

Pr. In Hoder's hand the Heroe's doom:
His Brother sends him to the tomb.
Now my weary lips I close;
Leave me, leave me to repose.

O. Prophetess, my spell obey,
Once again arise, and say,
Who th' Avenger of his guilt,
By whom shall Hoder's blood be spilt?

Pr. In the caverns of the west,
By Odin's fierce embrace comprest,
A wond'rous Boy shall Rinda bear,
Who ne'er shall comb his raven-hair,
Nor wash his visage in the stream,
Nor see the sun's departing beam,
Till he on Hoder's corse shall smile
Flaming on the fun'ral pile.
Now my weary lips I close:
Leave me, leave me to repose.

O. Yet awhile my call obey;
Prophetess, awake, and say,
What Virgins these, in speechless woe,
That bend to earth their solemn brow,
That their flaxen tresses tear,
And snowy veils, that float in air.
Tell me, whence their sorrows rose:
Then I leave thee to repose.

Pr. Ha! no Traveller art thou,
King of Men, I know thee now;
Mightiest of a mighty line——

O. No boding Maid of skill divine
Art thou, nor Prophetess of good;   85
But Mother of the giant-brood!

Pr. Hie thee hence, and boast at home,
That never shall Enquirer come
To break my iron-sleep again;
Till Lok has burst his tenfold chain;   90
Never, till substantial Night
Has reassum'd her ancient right;
Till wrapt in flames, in ruin hurl'd,
Sinks the fabric of the world.

THE TRIUMPHS OF OWEN.

OWEN'S praise demands my song,
Owen swift, and Owen strong;
Fairest flower of Roderic's stem,
Gwyneth's shield, and Britain's gem.
He nor heaps his brooded stores,   5
Nor on all profusely pours;
Lord of every regal art,
Liberal hand, and open heart.

Big with hosts of mighty name,
Squadrons three against him came;   10
This the force of Eirin hiding,
Side by side as proudly riding,
On her shadow long and gay
Lochlin plows the watry way;

THE TRIUMPHS OF OWEN.

There the Norman sails afar 15
Catch the winds, and join the war :
Black and huge along they sweep,
Burthens of the angry deep.

Dauntless on his native sands
The Dragon-Son of Mona stands ; 20
In glitt'ring arms and glory drest,
High he rears his ruby crest.
There the thund'ring strokes begin,
There the press, and there the din ;
Talymalfra's rocky shore 25
Echoing to the battle's roar.
[Check'd by the torrent-tide of blood,
Backward Meinai rolls his flood ;
While, heap'd his master's feet around,
Prostrate warriors gnaw the ground.] 30
Where his glowing eye-balls turn,
Thousand Banners round him burn :
Where he points his purple spear,
Hasty, hasty Rout is there,
Marking with indignant eye 35
Fear to stop, and shame to fly,
There Confusion, Terror's child,
Conflict fierce, and Ruin wild,
Agony, that pants for breath,
Despair and honourable death. 40

*   *   *

ELEGY WRITTEN IN A COUNTRY CHURCH-YARD.

THE Curfew tolls the knell of parting day,
The lowing herd wind slowly o'er the lea,
The plowman homeward plods his weary way,
And leaves the world to darkness and to me.

Now fades the glimmering landscape on the sight, 5
And all the air a solemn stillness holds,
Save where the beetle wheels his droning flight,
And drowsy tinklings lull the distant folds:

Save that from yonder ivy-mantled tow'r
The mopeing owl does to the moon complain 10
Of such as, wand'ring near her secret bow'r,
Molest her ancient solitary reign.

Beneath those rugged elms, that yew-tree's shade,
Where heaves the turf in many a mould'ring heap,
Each in his narrow cell for ever laid, 15
The rude Forefathers of the hamlet sleep.

The breezy call of incense-breathing Morn,
The swallow twitt'ring from the straw-built shed,
The cock's shrill clarion, or the echoing horn,
No more shall rouse them from their lowly bed. 20

For them no more the blazing hearth shall burn,
Or busy housewife ply her evening care:
No children run to lisp their sire's return,
Or climb his knees the envied kiss to share.

Oft did the harvest to their sickle yield, 25
Their furrow oft the stubborn glebe has broke :
How jocund did they drive their team afield!
How bow'd the woods beneath their sturdy stroke!

Let not Ambition mock their useful toil,
Their homely joys, and destiny obscure ; 30
Nor Grandeur hear with a disdainful smile
The short and simple annals of the poor.

The boast of heraldry, the pomp of pow'r,
And all that beauty, all that wealth e'er gave,
Awaits alike th' inevitable hour. 35
The paths of glory lead but to the grave.

Nor you, ye Proud, impute to These the fault,
If Mem'ry o'er their Tomb no Trophies raise,
Where through the long-drawn isle and fretted vault
The pealing anthem swells the note of praise. 40

Can storied urn or animated bust
Back to its mansion call the fleeting breath?
Can Honour's voice provoke the silent dust,
Or Flatt'ry soothe the dull cold ear of death?

Perhaps in this neglected spot is laid 45
Some heart once pregnant with celestial fire ;
Hands, that the rod of empire might have sway'd,
Or wak'd to extasy the living lyre.

But Knowledge to their eyes her ample page
Rich with the spoils of time did ne'er unroll ; 50
Chill Penury repress'd their noble rage,
And froze the genial current of the soul.

Full many a gem of purest ray serene,
  The dark unfathom'd caves of ocean bear:
Full many a flower is born to blush unseen,   55
  And waste its sweetness on the desert air.

Some village-Hampden that with dauntless breast
  The little Tyrant of his fields withstood,
Some mute inglorious Milton here may rest,
  Some Cromwell guiltless of his country's blood.   60

Th' applause of list'ning senates to command,
  The threats of pain and ruin to despise,
To scatter plenty o'er a smiling land,
  And read their hist'ry in a nation's eyes,

Their lot forbad: nor circumscrib'd alone   65
  Their growing virtues, but their crimes confin'd;
Forbad to wade through slaughter to a throne,
  And shut the gates of mercy on mankind,

The struggling pangs of conscious truth to hide,
  To quench the blushes of ingenuous shame,   70
Or heap the shrine of Luxury and Pride
  With incense kindled at the Muse's flame.

Far from the madding crowd's ignoble strife,
  Their sober wishes never learn'd to stray;
Along the cool sequester'd vale of life   75
  They kept the noiseless tenor of their way.

Yet ev'n these bones from insult to protect
  Some frail memorial still erected nigh,
With uncouth rhimes and shapeless sculpture deck'd,
  Implores the passing tribute of a sigh.   80

Their name, their years, spelt by th' unletter'd muse,
  The place of fame and elegy supply:
And many a holy text around she strews,
  That teach the rustic moralist to die.

For who to dumb Forgetfulness a prey,   85
  This pleasing anxious being e'er resign'd,
Left the warm precincts of the chearful day,
  Nor cast one longing ling'ring look behind?

On some fond breast the parting soul relies,
  Some pious drops the closing eye requires;   90
E'en from the tomb the voice of Nature cries,
  E'en in our Ashes live their wonted Fires.

For thee, who mindful of th' unhonour'd Dead,
  Dost in these lines their artless tale relate;
If chance, by lonely contemplation led,   95
  Some kindred Spirit shall inquire thy fate,—

Haply some hoary-headed Swain may say,
  'Oft have we seen him at the peep of dawn
Brushing with hasty steps the dews away
  To meet the sun-upon the upland lawn.   100

'There at the foot of yonder nodding beech,
  That wreathes its old fantastic roots so high,
His listless length at noontide would he stretch,
  And pore upon the brook that babbles by.

'Hard by yon wood, now smiling as in scorn,   105
  Mutt'ring his wayward fancies he would rove,
Now drooping, woeful-wan, like one forlorn,
  Or craz'd with care, or cross'd in hopeless love.

'One morn I miss'd him on the custom'd hill,
    Along the heath, and near his fav'rite tree;   110
Another came; nor yet beside the rill,
    Nor up the lawn, nor at the wood was he:

'The next, with dirges due in sad array
    Slow thro' the church-way path we saw him borne.
Approach and read (for thou cans't read) the lay,   115
    Grav'd on the stone beneath yon aged thorn.'

THE EPITAPH.

Here rests his head upon the lap of Earth
    A Youth, to Fortune and to Fame unknown.
Fair Science frown'd not on his humble birth,
    And Melancholy mark'd him for her own.   120

Large was his bounty, and his soul sincere,
    Heav'n did a recompence as largely send:
He gave to Mis'ry all he had, a tear,
    He gain'd from Heav'n ('twas all he wish'd) a friend.

No farther seek his merits to disclose,   125
    Or draw his frailties from their dread abode,
(There they alike in trembling hope repose,)
    The bosom of his Father and his God.

A LONG STORY.

IN Britain's Isle, no matter where,
  An ancient pile of buildings stands :
The Huntingdons and Hattons there
  Employ'd the power of Fairy hands.

To raise the cieling's fretted height,   5
  Each pannel in achievements cloathing,
Rich windows that exclude the light,
  And passages, that lead to nothing.

Full oft within the spatious walls,
  When he had fifty winters o'er him,   10
My grave Lord-Keeper led the Brawls ;
  The Seal, and Maces, danc'd before him.

His bushy beard, and shoe-strings green,
  His high-crown'd hat, and sattin-doublet,
Mov'd the stout heart of England's Queen, 15
  Tho' Pope and Spaniard could not trouble it.

What, in the very first beginning!
  Shame of the versifying tribe !
Your Hist'ry whither are you spinning ?
  Can you do nothing but describe ?   20

A House there is, (and that's enough)
  From whence one fatal morning issues
A brace of Warriors, not in buff,
  But rustling in their silks and tissues.

A LONG STORY.

The first came cap-a-pee from France   25
  Her conqu'ring destiny fulfilling,
Whom meaner Beauties eye askance,
  And vainly ape her art of killing.

The other Amazon kind Heaven
  Had arm'd with spirit, wit, and satire :   30
But Cobham had the polish given
  And tip'd her arrows with good-nature.

To celebrate her eyes, her air——
  Coarse panegyricks would but teaze her.
Melissa is her Nom de Guerre.   35
  Alas, who would not wish to please her!

With bonnet blue and capucine,
  And aprons long they hid their armour,
And veil'd their weapons bright and keen
  In pity to the country-farmer.   40

Fame, in the shape of Mr. Purt,
  (By this time all the Parish know it)
Had told, that thereabouts there lurk'd
  A wicked Imp they call a Poet,

Who prowl'd the country far and near,   45
  Bewitch'd the children of the peasants,
Dried up the cows, and lam'd the deer,
  And suck'd the eggs, and kill'd the pheasants.

My Lady heard their joint petition,
  Swore by her coronet and ermine,   50
She'd issue out her high commission
  To rid the manour of such vermin.

The Heroines undertook the task,
    Thro' lanes unknown, o'er stiles they ventur'd,
Rap'd at the door, nor stay'd to ask,   55
    But bounce into the parlour enter'd.

The trembling family they daunt,
    They flirt, they sing, they laugh, they tattle,
Rummage his Mother, pinch his Aunt,
    And up stairs in a whirlwind rattle.   60

Each hole and cupboard they explore,
    Each creek and cranny of his chamber,
Run hurry-skurry round the floor,
    And o'er the bed and tester clamber,

Into the Drawers and China pry,   65
    Papers and books, a huge Imbroglio!
Under a tea-cup he might lie,
    Or creased, like dogs-ears, in a folio.

On the first marching of the troops
    The Muses, hopeless of his pardon,   70
Convey'd him underneath their hoops
    To a small closet in the garden.

So Rumor says. (Who will, believe.)
    But that they left the door a-jarr,
Where, safe and laughing in his sleeve,   75
    He heard the distant din of war.

Short was his joy. He little knew
    The power of Magick was no fable.
Out of the window, whisk, they flew,
    But left a spell upon the table.   80

The words too eager to unriddle,
The Poet felt a strange disorder:
Transparent birdlime form'd the middle,
And chains invisible the border.

So cunning was the Apparatus,   85
The powerful pothooks did so move him,
That will he, nill he, to the Great-house
He went, as if the Devil drove him.

Yet on his way (no sign of grace,
For folks in fear are apt to pray)   90
To Phoebus he prefer'd his case,
And beg'd his aid that dreadful day.

The Godhead would have back'd his quarrel,
But with a blush on recollection
Own'd, that his quiver and his laurel   95
'Gainst four such eyes were no protection.

The Court was sate, the Culprit there;
Forth from their gloomy mansions creeping
The lady Janes and Joans repair,
And from the gallery stand peeping: 100

Such as in silence of the night
Come (sweep) along some winding entry
(Styack has often seen the sight)
Or at the chappel-door stand sentry;

In peaked hoods and mantles tarnish'd,   105
Sour visages, enough to scare ye,
High Dames of honour once, that garnish'd
The drawing-room of fierce Queen Mary.

A LONG STORY.

The Peeress comes. The Audience stare,
   And doff their hats with due submission: 110
She curtsies, as she takes her chair,
   To all the People of condition.

The bard, with many an artful fib,
   Had in imagination fenc'd him,
Disprov'd the arguments of Squib, 115
   And all that Groom could urge against him.

But soon his rhetorick forsook him,
   When he the solemn hall had seen;
A sudden fit of ague shook him,
   He stood as mute as poor Macleane. 120

Yet something he was heard to mutter,
   'How in the park beneath an old-tree,
(Without design to hurt the butter,
   Or any malice to the poultry,)

'He once or twice had pen'd a sonnet; 125
   Yet hop'd, that he might save his bacon:
Numbers would give their oaths upon it,
   He ne'er was for a conj'rer taken.'

The ghostly Prudes with hagged face
   Already had condemn'd the sinner. 130
My Lady rose, and with a grace——
   She smiled, and bid him come to dinner.

'Jesu-Maria! Madam Bridget,
   Why, what can the Viscountess mean?'
(Cried the square Hoods in woful fidget) 135
   'The times are alter'd quite and clean!

'Decorum's turn'd to mere civility;
Her air and all her manners shew it.
Commend me to her affability!
Speak to a Commoner and Poet!' 140

[Here 500 Stanzas are lost.]

And so God save our noble King,
  And guard us from long-winded Lubbers,
That to eternity would sing,
  And keep my Lady from her Rubbers.

THE INSTALLATION ODE.

I. AIR.

'HENCE, avaunt, ('tis holy ground)
  Comus, and his midnight crew,
And Ignorance with looks profound,
  And dreaming Sloth of pallid hue,
Mad Sedition's cry profane, 5
Servitude that hugs her chain,
Nor in these consecrated bowers,
Let painted Flatt'ry hide her serpent-train in flowers.

CHORUS.

Nor Envy base, nor creeping Gain,
Dare the Muse's walk to stain, 10
While bright-eyed Science watches round:
Hence, away, 'tis holy ground!

II. Recitative.

From yonder realms of empyrean day
Bursts on my ear th' indignant lay :
    There sit the sainted sage, the bard divine,   15
    The few, whom genius gave to shine
Thro' every unborn age, and undiscover'd clime.
    Rapt in celestial transport they :
    Yet hither oft a glance from high
    They send of tender sympathy   20
To bless the place, where on their opening soul
    First the genuine ardour stole.
'Twas Milton struck the deep-ton'd shell,
And, as the choral warblings round him swell,
Meek Newton's self bends from his state sublime,   25
And nods his hoary head, and listens to the rhyme.

III. Air.

    'Ye brown o'er-arching groves,
    That contemplation loves,
Where willowy Camus lingers with delight!
    Oft at the blush of dawn   30
    I trod your level lawn,
Oft woo'd the gleam of Cynthia silver-bright
In cloisters dim, far from the haunts of Folly,
With Freedom by my side, and soft-eyed Melancholy.'

IV. Recitative.

But hark! the portals sound, and pacing forth   35
    With solemn steps and slow,
High potentates, and dames of royal birth,
And mitred fathers in long order go :

THE INSTALLATION ODE.

Great Edward, with the lilies on his brow
    From haughty Gallia torn,   40
And sad Chatillon, on her bridal morn
That wept her bleeding Love, and princely Clare,
And Anjou's heroine, and the paler rose,
The rival of her crown and of her woes,
    And either Henry there,   45
The murder'd saint and the majestic lord,
    That broke the bonds of Rome.
(Their tears, their little triumphs o'er,
Their human passions now no more,
Save Charity, that glows beyond the tomb.)   50

ACCOMPANIED.

All that on Granta's fruitful plain
Rich streams of regal bounty pour'd,
And bad these awful fanes and turrets rise,
To hail their Fitzroy's festal morning come;
    And thus they speak in soft accord   55
The liquid language of the skies:

V. QUARTETTO.

'What is grandeur, what is power?
Heavier toil, superior pain.
What the bright reward we gain?
The grateful memory of the good.   60
Sweet is the breath of vernal shower,
The bee's collected treasures sweet,
Sweet music's melting fall, but sweeter yet
The still small voice of gratitude.'

THE INSTALLATION ODE.

VI. RECITATIVE.

Foremost and leaning from her golden cloud 65
The venerable Marg'ret see!
'Welcome, my noble son, (she cries aloud)
  To this, thy kindred train, and me:
Pleas'd in thy lineaments we trace
A Tudor's fire, a Beaufort's grace.' 70

AIR.

'Thy liberal heart, thy judging eye,
The flow'r unheeded shall descry,
And bid it round heav'n's altars shed
The fragrance of its blushing head:
Shall raise from earth the latent gem 75
To glitter on the diadem.'

VII. RECITATIVE.

'Lo! Granta waits to lead her blooming band,
  Not obvious, not obtrusive, she
No vulgar praise, ño venal incense flings;
  Nor dares with courtly tongue refin'd, 80
Profane thy inborn royalty of mind:
  She reveres herself and thee.
With modest pride to grace thy youthful brow,
The laureate wreath, that Cecil wore, she brings,
  And to thy just, thy gentle hand, 85
  Submits the fasces of her sway,
While spirits blest above and men below
Join with glad voice the loud symphonious lay.'

VIII. GRAND CHORUS.

'Thro' the wild waves as they roar,
With watchful eye and dauntless mien,   90
Thy steady course of honour keep,
Nor fear the rocks, nor seek the shore:
The star of Brunswick smiles serene,
And gilds the horrors of the deep.'

SONNET

ON THE DEATH OF RICHARD WEST.

IN vain to me the smileing Mornings shine,
    And redning Phœbus lifts his golden Fire:
The Birds in vain their amorous Descant joyn;
    Or chearful Fields resume their green Attire:
These Ears, alas! for other Notes repine,   5
    A different Object do these Eyes require:
My lonely Anguish melts no Heart but mine;
    And in my Breast the imperfect Joys expire.
Yet Morning smiles the busy Race to chear,
    And new-born Pleasure brings to happier Men: 10
The Fields to all their wonted Tribute bear;
    To warm their little Loves the Birds complain:
I fruitless mourn to him that cannot hear,
    And weep the more because I weep in vain.

HYMN TO IGNORANCE.

A FRAGMENT.

HAIL, horrors, hail! ye ever gloomy bowers,
Ye gothic fanes, and antiquated towers,
Where rushy Camus' slowly-winding flood
Perpetual draws his humid train of mud:
Glad I revisit thy neglected reign, 5
Oh take me to thy peaceful shade again.
But chiefly thee, whose influence breathed from high
Augments the native darkness of the sky;
Ah, ignorance! soft salutary power!
Prostrate with filial reverence I adore. 10
Thrice hath Hyperion roll'd his annual race,
Since weeping I forsook thy fond embrace.
Oh say, successful dost thou still oppose
Thy leaden ægis 'gainst our ancient foes?
Still stretch, tenacious of thy right divine, 15
The massy sceptre o'er thy slumb'ring line?
And dews Lethean through the land dispense
To steep in slumbers each benighted sense?
If any spark of wit's delusive ray
Break out, and flash a momentary day, 20
With damp, cold touch forbid it to aspire,
And huddle up in fogs the dang'rous fire.
  Oh say—she hears me not, but, careless grown,
Lethargic nods upon her ebon throne.
Goddess! awake, arise! alas, my fears! 25
Can powers immortal feel the force of years?
Not thus of old, with ensigns wide unfurl'd,
She rode triumphant o'er the vanquish'd world;

Fierce nations own'd her unresisted might,
And all was ignorance, and all was night.   30
  Oh! sacred¹ age! Oh! times for ever lost!
(The schoolman's glory, and the churchman's boast,)
For ever gone—yet still to fancy new,
Her rapid wings the transient scene pursue,
And bring the buried ages back to view.   35
  High on her car, behold the grandam ride
Like old Sesostris with barbaric pride;
* * * a team of harness'd monarchs bend

     *   *   *   *

STANZAS TO MR. RICHARD BENTLEY.

IN silent gaze the tuneful choir among,
  Half pleas'd, half blushing, let the Muse admire,
While Bentley leads her sister-art along,
  And bids the pencil answer to the lyre.

See, in their course, each transitory thought   5
  Fix'd by his touch a lasting essence take;
Each dream, in fancy's airy colouring wrought
  To local symmetry and life awake!

The tardy rhymes that us'd to linger on,
  To censure cold, and negligent of fame,   10
In swifter measures animated run,
  And catch a lustre from his genuine flame.

Ah! could they catch his strength, his easy grace,
  His quick creation, his unerring line;
The energy of Pope they might efface,   15
  And Dryden's harmony submit to mine.

But not to one in this benighted age
  Is that diviner inspiration giv'n,
That burns in Shakespeare's or in Milton's page,
  The pomp and prodigality of heav'n.   20

As when conspiring in the diamond's blaze,
  The meaner gems that singly charm the sight,
Together dart their intermingled rays,
  And dazzle with a luxury of light.

Enough for me, if to some feeling breast   25
  My lines a secret sympathy * *
And as their pleasing influence * * *
  A sigh of soft reflection * * *

ODE ON THE PLEASURE ARISING FROM VICISSITUDE.

FRAGMENT.

Now the golden Morn aloft
  Waves her dew-bespangled wing,
With vermeil-cheek and whisper soft
  She woo's the tardy spring:
Till April starts, and calls around   5
The sleeping fragrance from the ground;
And lightly o'er the living scene
Scatters his freshest, tenderest green.

New-born flocks, in rustic dance,
  Frisking ply their feeble feet ; 10
Forgetful of their wintry trance,
  The Birds his presence greet :
But chief, the Sky-lark warbles high
  His trembling thrilling ecstasy ;
And, lessening from the dazzled sight, 15
Melts into air and liquid light.

Rise, my soul! on wings of fire,
  Rise the rapturous choir among ;
Hark! 'tis nature strikes the lyre,
  And leads the general song : 20

Yesterday the sullen year
  Saw the snowy whirlwind fly ;
Mute was the musick of the air,
  The Herd stood drooping by :
Their raptures now that wildly flow, · 25
No yesterday, nor morrow know ;
'Tis man alone that Joy descries
With forward and reverted eyes.

Smiles on past Misfortune's brow
  Soft Reflection's hand can trace ; 30
And o'er the cheek of Sorrow throw
  A melancholy grace ;
While Hope prolongs our happier hour,
Or deepest shades, that dimly lower
And blacken round our weary way, 35
Gilds with a gleam of distant day.

Still, where rosy Pleasure leads,
  See a kindred Grief pursue ;
Behind the steps that Misery treads,
  Approaching Comfort view : 40
The hues of Bliss more brightly glow,
Chastised by sabler tints of woe ;
And blended form, with artful strife,
The strength and harmony of Life.

See the Wretch, that long has tost 45
  On the thorny bed of Pain,
At length repair his vigour lost,
  And breathe and walk again :
The meanest flowret of the vale,
The simplest note that swells the gale, 50
The common Sun, the air, the skies,
To him are opening Paradise.

Humble quiet builds her cell,
  Near the source whence Pleasure flows :
 She eyes the clear chrystalline well, 55
  And tastes it as it goes.
Far below,   the crowd.

Where broad and turbulent it grows
            with resistless sweep
They perish in the boundless deep. 60

Mark where Indolence and Pride,

Softly rolling, side by side,
  Their dull, but daily round.

EPITAPH ON MRS. JANE CLERKE.

Lo! where the silent marble weeps,
A friend, a wife, a mother sleeps:
A heart, within whose sacred cell
The peaceful virtues lov'd to dwell.
Affection warm, and faith sincere,   5
And soft humanity were there.
In agony, in death resign'd,
She felt the wound she left behind,
Her infant image here below,
Sits smiling on a father's woe: 10
Whom what awaits, while yet he strays
Along the lonely vale of days?
A pang, to secret sorrow dear;
A sigh; an unavailing tear;
Till time shall every grief remove,   15
With life, with memory, and with love.

EPITAPH ON A CHILD.

Here, freed from pain, secure from misery, lies
A child, the darling of his parents' eyes:
A gentler Lamb ne'er sported on the plain,
A fairer flower will never bloom again:
Few were the days allotted to his breath;
Now let him sleep in peace his night of death.

SKETCH OF HIS OWN CHARACTER.

WRITTEN IN 1761, AND FOUND IN ONE OF HIS
POCKET-BOOKS.

TOO poor for a bribe, and too proud to importune;
He had not the method of making a fortune:
Could love, and could hate, so was thought somewhat odd;
No very great wit, he believed in a God:
A place or a pension he did not desire,
But left church and state to Charles Townshend and Squire.

EPITAPH ON SIR WILLIAM WILLIAMS.

HERE, foremost in the dangerous paths of fame,
  Young Williams fought for England's fair renown;
His mind each Muse, each Grace adorn'd his frame,
  Nor envy dar'd to view him with a frown.

At Aix, his voluntary sword he drew, 5
  There first in blood his infant honour seal'd;
From fortune, pleasure, science, love, he flew,
  And scorn'd repose when Britain took the field.

With eyes of flame, and cool undaunted breast,
  Victor he stood on Bellisle's rocky steeps— 10
Ah, gallant youth! this marble tells the rest,
  Where melancholy friendship bends, and weeps.

THE DEATH OF HOEL.

AN ODE. SELECTED FROM THE GODODIN.

HAD I but the torrent's might,
With headlong rage and wild affright
Upon Deïra's squadrons hurl'd
To rush, and sweep them from the world!

Too, too secure in youthful pride, 5
By them, my friend, my Hoel, died,
Great Cian's son: of Madoc old
He ask'd no heaps of hoarded gold;
Alone in nature's wealth array'd,
He ask'd and had the lovely maid. 10

To Cattraeth's vale in glitt'ring row
Thrice two hundred warriors go:
Every warrior's manly neck
Chains of regal honour deck,
Wreath'd in many a golden link: 15
From the golden cup they drink
Nectar that the bees produce,
Or the grape's extatic juice.
Flush'd with mirth and hope they burn:
But none from Cattraeth's vale return, 20
Save Aëron brave, and Conan strong,
(Bursting through the bloody throng)
And I, the meanest of them all,
That live to weep and sing their fall.

CARADOC.

HAVE ye seen the dusky boar,
Or the bull, with sullen roar,
On surrounding foes advance?
So Caradoc bore his lance.

CONAN.

CONAN'S name, my lay, rehearse,
Build to him the lofty verse,
Sacred tribute of the bard,
Verse, the hero's sole reward.
As the flame's devouring force ;   5
As the whirlwind in its course;
As the thunder's fiery stroke,
Glancing on the shiver'd oak ;
Did the sword of Conan mow
The crimson harvest of the foe.   10

IMPROMPTU,

SUGGESTED BY A VIEW, IN 1766, OF THE SEAT AND RUINS
OF A DECEASED NOBLEMAN, AT KINGSGATE, KENT.

OLD, and abandon'd by each venal friend,
  Here Holland form'd the pious resolution
To smuggle a few years, and strive to mend
  A broken character and constitution.

On this congenial spot he fix'd his choice;   5
  Earl Goodwin trembled for his neighbouring sand;
Here sea-gulls scream, and cormorants rejoice,
  And mariners, though shipwreck'd, dread to land.

Here reign the blustering North and blighting East,
  No tree is heard to whisper, bird to sing;   10
Yet Nature could not furnish out the feast,
  Art he invokes new horrors still to bring.

Here mouldering fanes and battlements arise,
  Turrets and arches nodding to their fall,
Unpeopled monast'ries delude our eyes,   15
  And mimic desolation covers all.

'Ah!' said the sighing peer, 'had Bute been true,
  Nor Mungo's, Rigby's, Bradshaw's friendship vain,
Far better scenes than these had blest our view,
  And realis'd the beauties which we feign: 20

'Purg'd by the sword, and purified by fire,
  Then had we seen proud London's hated walls;
Owls would have hooted in St. Peter's choir,
  And foxes stunk and litter'd in St. Paul's.'

AMATORY LINES.

WITH beauty, with pleasure surrounded, to languish—
To weep without knowing the cause of my anguish:
To start from short slumbers, and wish for the morning—
To close my dull eyes when I see it returning;
Sighs sudden and frequent, looks ever dejected—
Words that steal from my tongue, by no meaning connected!
Ah! say, Fellow-swains, how these symptoms befell me?
They smile, but reply not—Sure Delia will tell me!

SONG.

THYRSIS, when we parted, swore
   Ere the spring he would return—
Ah! what means yon violet flower!
   And the buds that deck the thorn!
'Twas the Lark that upward sprung!   5
'Twas the Nightingale that sung!

Idle notes! untimely green!
   Why this unavailing haste?
Western gales and skies serene
   Speak not always winter past.   10
Cease, my doubts, my fears to move,
Spare the honour of my love.

FROM PROPERTIUS.

LIB. II. ELEG. I.

To Mæcenas.

YOU ask, why thus my Loves I still rehearse,
Whence the soft Strain and ever-melting Verse?
From Cynthia all that in my numbers shines;
She is my Genius, she inspires the Lines;
No Phœbus else, no other Muse I know,　　　5
She tunes my easy Rhime, and gives the Lay to flow.
If the loose Curls around her Forehead play,
Or lawless, o'er their Ivory Margin stray:
If the thin Coan Web her Shape reveal,
And half disclose those Limbs it should conceal;　10
Of those loose Curls, that Ivory front I write;
Of the dear Web whole Volumes I indite:
Or if to Musick she the Lyre awake,
That the soft Subject of my Song I make,
And sing with what a careless Grace she flings　15
Her artful hand across the sounding Strings.
If sinking into Sleep she seem to close
Her languid Lids, I favour her repose.
With lulling Notes, and thousand beauties see
That Slumber brings to aid my Poetry.　　　20
When, less averse, and yielding to Desires,
She half accepts, and half rejects, my Fires,
While to retain the envious Lawn she tries,
And struggles to elude my longing Eyes,
The fruitful Muse from that auspicious Night　25
Dates the long Iliad of the amorous Fight.

In brief whate'er she do, or say, or look,
'Tis ample Matter for a Lover's Book;
And many a copious Narrative you'll see
Big with the important Nothing's History. 30
Yet would the Tyrant Love permit me raise
My feeble Voice, to sound the Victor's Praise,
To paint the Hero's Toil, the Ranks of War,
The laurell'd Triumph and the sculptured Carr;
No Giant Race, no Tumult of the Skies, 35
No Mountain-Structures in my Verse should rise,
Nor Tale of Thebes, nor Ilium there should be,
Nor how the Persian trod the indignant Sea;
Not Marius' Cimbrian Wreaths would I relate,
Nor lofty Carthage struggleing with her Fate. 40
Here should Augustus great in Arms appear,
And thou Mæcenas, be my second Care;
Here Mutina from flames and famine free,
And there the ensanguined Wave of Sicily,
And scepter'd Alexandria's captive Shore, 45
And sad Philippi, red with Roman Gore:
Then, while the vaulted Skies loud Ios rend,
In golden Chains should loaded Monarchs bend,
And hoary Nile with pensive Aspect seem
To mourn the Glories of his sevenfold Stream, 50
While Prows, that late in fierce Encounter mett,
Move through the Sacred Way and vainly threat,
Thee too the Muse should consecrate to Fame,
And with her Garlands weave thy ever-faithful Name.
 But nor Callimachus' enervate Strain 55
May tell of Jove, and Phlegra's blasted Plain;
Nor I with unaccustom'd Vigour trace
Back to it's Source divine the Julian Race.

Sailors to tell of Winds and Seas delight,
The Shepherd of his flocks, the Soldier of the Fight,   60
A milder Warfare I in Verse display;
Each in his proper Art should waste the Day,
Nor thou my gentle Calling disapprove,
To die is glorious in the Bed of Love.
  Happy the Youth, and not unknown to Fame,   65
Whose heart has never felt a second flame.
Oh, might that envied Happiness be mine!
To Cynthia all my Wishes I confine;
Or if, alas! it be my Fate to try
Another Love, the quicker let me die: 70
But she, the Mistress of my faithful breast,
Has oft the Charms of Constancy confest,
Condemns her fickle Sexe's fond Mistake,
And hates the Tale of Troy for Helen's Sake.
Me from myself the soft Enchantress stole;   75
Ah! let her ever my Desires control,
Or if I fall the Victim of her Scorn,
From her loved Door may my pale Coarse be borne.
The Power of Herbs can other Harms remove,
And find a Cure for every Ill, but Love.   80
The Melian's Hurt Machaon could repair,
Heal the slow Chief, and send again to War;
To Chiron Phœnix owed his long-lost Sight,
And Phœbus' Son recall'd Androgeon to the Light.
Here Arts are vain, e'en Magic here must fail,   85
The powerful Mixture and the midnight Spell;
The Hand that can my captive heart release,
And to this bosom give its wonted Peace,
May the long Thirst of Tantalus allay,
Or drive the infernal Vulture from his Prey.   90

FROM DANTE. 85

For Ills unseen what Remedy is found?
Or who can probe the undiscover'd Wound?
The Bed avails not, nor the leeche's Care,
Nor changing Skies can hurt, nor sultry Air.
'Tis hard th' elusive Symptoms to explore: 95
To-day the Lover walks, to-morrow is no more;
A train of mourning Friends attend his Pall,
And wonder at the sudden Funeral.
    When then my Fates that breath they gave shall claim,
And the short Marble but preserve a Name, 100
A little Verse my All that shall remain;
Thy passing Courser's slacken'd Speed restrain;
(Thou envied Honour of thy Poet's Days,
Of all our Youth the Ambition and the Praise!)
Then to my quiet Urn awhile draw near, 105
And say, while o'er the Place You drop the Tear,
Love and the Fair were of his Life the Pride;
He lived, while she was kind; and when she frown'd, he died.

April, 1742.

FROM DANTE.

CANTO 33 DELL' INFERNO.

FROM his dire Food the griesly Fellon raised
His Gore-dyed Lips, which on the clotter'd Locks
Of th' half devoured Head he wiped, and thus
Began. Would'st thou revive the deep Despair,
The Anguish, that unutter'd nathless wrings 5
My inmost Heart? yet if the telling may

Beget the Traitour's Infamy, whom thus
I ceaseless gnaw insatiate; thou shalt see me
At once give loose to Utterance, and to Tears.
 I know not, who thou art; nor on what Errand 10
Sent hither: but a Florentine my Ear,
Won by thy Tongue, declares thee. Know, thou seest
In me Count Ugolino, and Ruggieri,
Pisa's perfidious Prelate this: now hear
My Wrongs, and from them judge of my Revenge. 15
 That I did trust him, that I was betray'd
By trusting, and by Treachery slain, it rekes not
That I advise thee. That which yet remains
To thee and all unknown (a horrid Tale)
The Bitterness of Death, I shall unfold. 20
Attend, and say if he have injured me.
 Thro' a small crevice opening, what scant Light
That grim and antique Tower admitted (since
Of me the Tower of Famine hight, and known
To many a Wretch) already 'gan the Dawn 25
To send: the whilst I slumb'ring lay, and Sleep
Prophetic of my Woes with direful Hand
Oped the dark Veil of Fate. I saw methought
Towards Pisa's Mount, that intercepts the View
Of Lucca, chas'd by Hell-hounds gaunt and bloody 30
A Wolf full-grown; with fleet and equal Speed
His young ones ran beside him. Lanfrance there
And Sigismundo, and Gualandi rode
Amain, my deadly Foes! headed by this
The deadliest. He their Chief, the foremost He 35
Flash'd to pursue, and chear the eager Cry:
Nor long endur'd the Chase: the panting Sire
Of strength bereft, his helpless offspring soon

FROM DANTE.

O'erta'en beheld, and in their trembling Flanks
The hungry Pack their sharp-set Fangs embrued. 40
The Morn had scarce commenc'd, when I awoke:
My Children (they were with me) sleep as yet
Gave not to know their Sum of Misery,
But yet in low and uncompleated Sounds
I heard 'em wail for Bread. Oh! thou art cruel, 45
Or Thou dost mourn to think, what my poor Heart
Foresaw, foreknew: oh! if thou weep not now,
Where are thy Tears? too soon they had aroused 'em
Sad with the Fears of Sleep, and now the Hour
Of timely Food approach'd; when at the Gate 50
Below I heard the dreadful Clash of Bars,
And fast'ning Bolts: then on my Children's Eyes
Speechless my Sight I fix'd, nor wept, for all
Within was Stone: they wept, unhappy Boys!
They wept, and first my little dear Anselmo 55
Cried, Father, why, why do you gaze so sternly?
What would you have? yet wept I not, or answer'd
All that whole Day, or the succeeding Night
Till a new Sun arose with weakly Gleam,
And wan, such as mought entrance find within 60
That House of Woe. But oh! when I beheld
My Sons, and in four Faces saw my own
Despair reflected, either Hand I gnaw'd
For Anguish, which they construed Hunger; straight
Ariseing all they cried, far less shall be 65
Our Suffering, Sir, if you resume your Gift;
These miserable Limbs with Flesh you cloath'd;
Take back, what once was yours. I swallow'd down
My struggling Sorrow, not to heighten theirs:
That Day, and yet another, mute we sate, 70

FROM DANTE.

And motionless ; oh Earth! couldst thou not gape
Quick to devour me? yet a fourth Day came
When Gaddo, at my Feet out-stretch'd, imploreing
In vain my Help, expir'd : e'er the sixth Morn
Had dawn'd, my other three before my Eyes   75
Died one by one ; I saw 'em fall ; I heard
Their doleful Cries ; for three days more I grop'd
About among their cold Remains (for then
Hunger had reft my Eye-sight) often calling
On their dear Names, that heard me now no more: 80
The fourth, what Sorrow could not, Hunger did.

He finish'd : Then with unrelenting Eye
Askaunce he turn'd him, hasty to renew
The hellish Feast, and rent his trembling Prey.

NOTES.

NOTES.

'IT is indisputably evident,' says Sir Joshua Reynolds, 'that a great part of every man's life must be employed in collecting materials for the exercise of genius. Invention, strictly speaking, is little more than a new combination of those images which have been previously gathered and deposited in the memory. Nothing can come of nothing. He who has laid up no materials, can produce no combinations. The more extensive therefore your acquaintance with the works of those who have excelled, the more extensive will be your powers of invention; and what may appear still more a paradox, the more original will be your conception.' These words apply to no poet more exactly than to Gray, whose diction is a mosaic of reminiscences from earlier authors, Greek and Latin, English and French, and who is nevertheless one of the most original writers in the language. In consequence of this, Gray has been habitually over-edited. The ingenuity of scholars has run wild in detecting instances in the older poets of lines, phrases, epithets and even particles, which Gray may be supposed to have imitated. In annotations of this kind there is the danger that the mind may be totally distracted from the original text by the copious and ingenious display of parallel passages. I have in the present edition desired to curb the instinct for discovering imitations, and have prepared the few notes which follow,—in which I have used without scruple the discoveries of earlier editors, Mason, Gilbert Wakefield, Luke, Mitford, Hales, and Rolfe,—with the sole intention of helping the student over any difficulty which he could reasonably be expected to meet with, and of indulging his curiosity with a restricted number of curious and typical parallelisms. Gray is not difficult to a careful reader. Actual obscurities of language or grammar are very few in him. But his poetry requires attention, sympathy, a mind attuned to lofty and rapid flights of the intelligence. It is hoped that the ensuing notes may serve the humble office of helping those who already possess these qualities.

ODE ON THE SPRING.

The Ode on the Spring exists in Gray's handwriting among the Stonehewer MSS. at Pembroke College, and is there entitled 'Noontide, An Ode.' At the end of the poem Gray has written :—'The beginning of June 1742, sent to Fav.: not knowing he was then Dead.' Favonius was the name given by Gray to Richard West, who died on the 1st of June 1742 at Hatfield. Gray had come down from London to Stoke in the last days of May, and must have written this poem almost immediately upon his arrival at West End, the house of his uncle, Mr. Rogers, afterwards the home of the poet's mother until her death. It was first published in Dodsley's Collection of Poems by several Hands, 1748, ii. 271, under the title 'Ode,' and as the first of Gray's Six Poems of 1753. The notes were first added by Gray in 1768.

l. 1. *the rosy-bosom'd Hours.* Cf. Milton, Comus, v. 984:
'The Graces, and the rosy-bosom'd Hours.'

l. 4. *purple year.* Purple is used here as a synonym of imperial, from the sumptuous and regal character of Summer.

l. 5. *Attic warbler.* The nightingale. Cf. Milton, Par. Reg. iv. 245:
'The Attic bird trills her thick-warbled notes.'
Milton borrowed the epithet from the Latin poets, with whom it is a commonplace.

l. 12. *A broader browner shade.* Pope, in Eloisa, v. 170, had said:
'And breathes a browner horror o'er the woods,'
and Dryden before him.

l. 14.   '... a bank
O'ercanopied with luscious woodbine.'
                Shakesp., Mids. Night's Dream. [Gray.]

ll. 19, 20. These lines were originally printed by Dodsley:
'How low, how indigent the Proud,
    How little are the Great!'
The variation, as Mason informs us, was subsequently made to avoid the point *little* and *great.*

l. 23. *peopled air.* Populous, that is, with birds and insects.

l. 25. *insect-youth.* This is perhaps an imitation of a phrase in Matthew Green's Grotto, *maggót-youth.* The whole turn of thought in the ode recalls the argument of Green's poem, as Gray himself perceived in later years.

NOTES. 93

l. 27. 'Nare per æstatem liquidam.'
Virgil, Georg. lib. iv. (59.) [Gray.]
l. 29. *trim* = dress. Sir Walter Scott, 'Seeing him just pass under the window in his woodland *trim*.'
l. 30. 'Sporting with quick glance,
Shew to the sun their waved coats drop'd with gold.'
Milton's Paradise Lost, book vii. (l. 410.) [Gray.]
l. 31. 'While insects from the threshold preach,' etc.
M. Green, in The Grotto. [Gray.]
l. 33. *they that creep and they that fly.* Cf. Pope, Essay on Man, l. 12 :
'Of all who blindly creep, or sightless soar.'

ODE ON THE DEATH OF A FAVOURITE CAT.

Several copies of this poem exist in Gray's handwriting. One in a letter to Walpole, dated March 1, 1747, one in a letter a few days later to Wharton, and one at Pembroke College. The subject was the death of one of Horace Walpole's favourite cats, Zara and Selima ('Selima, was it? or Fatima?'), which fell into a china bowl and was drowned. Walpole, after the death of Gray, placed the bowl on a pedestal at Strawberry Hill, with a few lines from this poem for its inscription. The Ode, which was written at Cambridge towards the end of February 1747, was first printed in Dodsley's Collection of Poems by several Hands, 1748, ii. 274, and forms the second piece in the 1753 edition of Gray's Six Poems.

l. 3. *that blow.* All the critics, from Dr. Johnson downwards, have pounced upon this redundancy. It is needless, of course, to say that the azure flowers blow, especially as, being painted porcelain blossoms, it is exactly what they do not do. It is as odd that Gray should have allowed this blemish to remain on his charming little poem, as that Wordsworth should have allowed the expression '*beautiful and fair*' to annoy the readers of his Ode on Intimations of Immortality.

ll. 4, 5. In the earliest MSS. and in the edition of 1748 the order of these lines is reversed.

l. 4. *tabby.* Gray uses this word as if it were synonymous with 'female cat'; but Selima cannot have been a tabby, if, as we presently read, she was a tortoiseshell. Tabby cats are those whose fur is of

94 ON A DISTANT PROSPECT OF ETON COLLEGE.

a cold brindled grey, like the surface of the rich watered silk from Bagdad, called '*attābi*', and in English *tabby*.

l. 13. *the tide*, i.e. the water in the bowl, which, of course, was absolutely stationary. This is, to be sure, used by Gray in a half-burlesque sense, but is yet a good instance of the conventional poetic language against which Cowper and Wordsworth rebelled.

l. 16. *Tyrian hue* = purple, because the best purple of antiquity was prepared at Tyre from the secretions of the Syrian murex.

l. 34. *No Dolphin came.* This refers to the legend of Arion, who threw himself into the sea from the deck of the Corinthian pirates, but was saved by a dolphin, which had approached the ship to listen to the strains of his lyre.

l. 42. *Nor all, that glisters, gold.* This line had passed into a proverb, and only the application of it belongs to Gray. In various forms it is to be found in Chaucer, Spenser, and many of our early poets. Shakespeare says
    'All that glisters is not gold.'
The Middle-English verb *glisteren* survives in this quotation and in Gray's line; otherwise *glitter* has taken its place.

ODE ON A DISTANT PROSPECT OF ETON COLLEGE.

This was the first of Gray's English productions which appeared in print: it was published anonymously as 'An Ode on a Distant Prospect of Eton College. London. Printed for R. Dodsley at Tully's Head in Pall-Mall; and sold by M. Cooper at the Globe in Pater-noster Row, 1747. (Price Sixpence, folio, pp. 8.)' According to a note by Gray at the close of the original MS. at Pembroke College, it was written 'at Stoke, Aug. 1742.' It appeared, still anonymously, in vol. ii, p. 267, of Dodsley's Collection of Poems in 1748, with no alterations of the text; and finally formed the third of the Six Poems of 1753. In Gray's MS. at Pembroke College, the title of this poem is, Ode on a Distant Prospect of Eton College, Windsor, and the adjacent Country. Through the courtesy of Dr. Grosart I am enabled to insert here a letter, never before published, from the poet Wordsworth to the Rev. John Moultrie, written in 1845 :—

My dear Sir,
  My Copy of the Ode in Gray's own hand-writing has 'Ah, happy Hills, ah pleasant Shade.' I wonder how Bentley could ever

have substituted 'Rills,' a reading which has no support in the context. The common copies read, a few lines below—'Full many a sprightly race,' Gray's own copy 'Full many a smileing (for so he spells the word).' Throughout the whole Poem the substantives are written in Capital Letters. He writes—'Fury-Passions,' and not, as commonly printed, the 'fury-passions.' What is the reason that our modern Compositors are so unwilling to employ Capital Letters?
believe me, my dear Sir,
faithfully yours,
RYDAL MOUNT, WM. WORDSWORTH.
Monday.

l. 3. *grateful Science.* Science is here used in its primary sense of knowledge, without restriction of nature. Cf. Pope:—
'Good sense, which only is the gift of Heaven,
Although no science, fairly worth the seven.'
That is to say, the seven scholastic sciences, grammar, logic, rhetoric, arithmetic, geometry, music, and astronomy. Gray represents knowledge as still worshipping the manes of Henry VI, who, by founding and endowing Eton College, made it her home and shrine.

l. 4. King Henry the Sixth, founder of the College. [Gray.]

l. 4. *Holy* shade. Henry VI. (1422-1471) was of a religious disposition, and his memory was in such favour at Rome that there was even a talk of his canonisation.

l. 15. *from ye blow.* A grammatical error, and now a vulgarism which should be carefully guarded against; *ye* is the nominative, and the objective must be *you*. Gray is here imitating Shakespeare, who uses the two forms without observing any distinction.

l. 19. 'And bees their honey *redolent of spring*,' Dryden's Fable on the Pythag. System. [Gray.] *redolent*, from 'redolens,' giving forth a sweet smell. Dr. Johnson thought the expression one that reaches a little beyond the utmost limits of the language. The epithet, however, occurs not only in Dryden, where Gray found it, but in the older English and Scotch poets. Cf. Alexander Scot:
'Wald God that I wer perigall
Vnder that *redolent* rose to rest.'

l. 21. *Say, father Thames.* Here again is a reminiscence of Matthew Green, who had said in his Grotto—
'Say, father Thames, whose gentle pace
Gives leave to view, what beauties grace
Your flowery banks, if you have seen.'

ON A DISTANT PROSPECT OF ETON COLLEGE.

l. 29, 30.   *To chase the rolling circle's speed,*
             Or urge the flying ball,
that is to say, to play at trundling hoops and at bat-trap-and-ball. In Bentley's drawing for this poem, made under Gray's eye, the schoolboys, dressed in nothing at all, are busy with bird-cages and hoops, while two youngsters are playing knurr-and-spell in the distance. In the foreground the water is occupied by bathers. There was little or no cricket or football played at Eton in the middle of the last century.

l. 37. *And unknown regions dare descry.* This line is borrowed bodily from Cowley, who, in his Pindarique Ode to Mr. Hobs, ll. 53-5, says:—
   'Thy nobler Vessel the vast Ocean tries,
   And nothing sees but Seas and skies,
   Till unknown Regions it descries.'

l. 40. *And snatch a fearful joy.* 'Fear is the strong passion; it is with fear that you must trifle, if you wish to taste the intensest joys of living.' R. L. Stevenson, The New Arabian Nights, i. 35.

l. 45. *buxom health.* Johnson objected to this expression. He says 'his epithet *buxom health* is not elegant; he seems not to understand the word.' But the meaning of *buxom* is 'gracious, lively, brisk,' and Gray may be confidently justified. Skeat says that the original meaning is 'pliable, obedient,' from *búgan*, to bend. It is constantly used in Gray's sense by the poets of the seventeenth century. Cf. Henry More, Psychozoia, ii. 31 (1647):—
   'As blith and buxom as was any lad
   Of one and twenty cloth'd in forrest green.'

l. 56. *The Ministers of human fate.* The original of this line has been found in the poems of Dr. William Broome, 1726, whose 'Melancholy: an Ode,' recalls this piece of Gray's in many respects. Broome says:—
   'With Cries we usher in our Birth,
   With Groans resign our transient Breath;
   While round, stern *Ministers of Fate,*
   Pain, and Disease, and Sorrow wait.'

l. 61. *fury Passions.* Cf. Pope, Essay on Man, iii. 167 :—
   'The fury Passions from that flood began.'

l. 64. *sculks,* to lurk or shirk behind. There is a Swedish verb *skolka*, to play truant. Both words are derived from the Icelandic *skjól*, a hiding-place.

l. 79. 'Madness laughing in his ireful mood.' Dryden's Fable of Palamon and Arcite. [Gray.]

l. 82. *a griesly troop.* For this odd spelling Gray is responsible. The word is *grisly*, 'horrible,' from the Anglo-Saxon *grýsan* to shudder. Cf. Skeat.

l. 83. *The painful family of Death.* Cf. Dryden, State of Innocence, Act 1

'Hate, Fear and Grief, *the family of Pain.*'

Gray was no doubt thinking of the *genus morborum* of the Latin poets.

l. 98. *Thought would destroy their paradise.* When Goethe was in Rome, he recommended the intellectual life to a young Italian. The answer was, 'Perché pensa? pensando s'invecchia,' why think, when it is thought that makes us old?

l. 99. *where ignorance is bliss.* Prior had said, in the Epistle to Montague,

'From ignorance our comfort flows,
The only wretched are the wise.'

But Davenant had stated the sentiment still more in Gray's rhythm in a 'song between two boys' in his tragi-comedy of The Just Italian, Act v. sc. 1 (1630):—

'Since Knowledge is but Sorrow's Spy,
It is not safe to know.'

HYMN TO ADVERSITY.

At the close of the MS. of this poem, then called an Ode, at Pembroke College, Gray has written 'At Stoke, Aug. 1742.' It was first printed in Dodsley's Collection, iv. 7, as 'Hymn to Adversity,' and again as the fifth of the Six Poems of 1753. It continued to hold this name during Gray's life, but in the first posthumous edition Mason restored the title 'Ode to Adversity.'

l. 1. *Daughter of Jove.* Ate ("Ατη), the goddess who avenges evil deeds by adversity, was the daughter of Zeus. She takes a prominent place in the tragedies of Æschylus, from one of which Gray selected a motto for one edition of this ode.

l. 5. *adamantine chain*, that is to say, 'unconquerable, unbreakable,' from the Greek ἀδάμας. The expression is common to most of the English poets, and may be traced to a phrase of Æschylus.

H

98   *THE PROGRESS OF POESY.*

l. 7. *purple Tyrants.* Cf. Horace, Ode I. 35, l. 12 :—
    'Purpurei metuunt tyranni.'
l. 9. *When first thy Sire.* The mythology here is of Gray's invention, and the *Virtue* he speaks of is the modern acceptation of the word, goodness, holiness, purity. The Roman *Virtus* was a personification of only one sort of goodness, namely, a manly courage in the battle-field. The construction of this quatrain may present some little difficulty. In prose it would run thus: 'When first thy sire design'd [i. e. determined] to send his darling child, Virtue, on earth, he confided the heavenly birth [i. e. the babe new-born from heaven] to thee, and bade [thee] to form her infant mind.'

l. 13. *Stern rugged Nurse.* The student should compare this hymn with Wordsworth's noble Ode to Duty, which was manifestly written in emulation of it, and in the same metre. Cf. l. 41 :—
    'Stern lawgiver! yet thou dost wear
    The Godhead's most benignant grace,' etc.

l. 22. *The summer Friend,* i. e. the friend whose affection will not outlast the sunshine of prosperity. Cf. Quarles, Sion's Elegies (1624), Threnodia I, xix. 3, 4 :—
    'Where shall I turne? shall I implore my friends?
    Ah! summer friendship with the summer ends.'

l. 35. *Gorgon terrors.* The youngest of the three Gorgons, Medusa, possessed this faculty, that by the mere presentment of her beautiful face she could turn the beholder into stone. This property her head retained after Perseus had slain her, and Athene therefore attached it to the centre of her ægis, a scaly goat-skin which served her as a shield, and by means of which she herself wielded *Gorgon terrors.*

l. 45. *The generous spark.* This was written about a year after Gray's quarrel with Horace Walpole, and I have suggested, in my Life of Gray (English Men of Letters Series, p. 64), that these lines are the record of a first return to those earlier feelings of affection to which Gray's pride and anger had so long made him insensible.

l. 47. *Exact* is here an adjective. 'Make me exact [i. e. precise, accurate] in scanning my own defects.'

THE PROGRESS OF POESY.

The Progress of Poesy was written at Cambridge in 1754. On the 26th of December Gray put the finishing touches to it, and sent it as 'an Ode in the Greek manner' to Dr. Wharton. It appeared, in company with the Bard, in a thin quarto volume:—'Odes by Mr. Gray. Φωνᾶντα συνετοῖσι.—Pindar, Olymp. II. Printed at Strawberry Hill, for R. and J. Dodsley in Pall Mall. MDCCLVII. Pp. 21. (Price One Shilling.)' This was published on the 8th of August 1757; it had an engraving of Strawberry Hill on the title-page, immediately below the citation from Pindar. The Progress of Poesy bears no other title in this first edition than Ode I. The notes were not in the edition of 1757, but were added by Gray in 1768, with this Advertisement:—' When the Author first published this and the following Ode, he was advised, even by his Friends, to subjoin some explanatory Notes, but had.too much respect for the understanding of his Readers to take that liberty.'

l. 1. *Awake.* Cowley, in his Davideis, had begun his Ode of David in a similar strain :—

'Awake, awake, my lyre,
And tell thy silent Master's humble tale.'
'Awake, my glory: awake, lute and harp.'
David's Psalms.

Pindar styles his own poetry, with its musical accompaniments, Αἰολῆὶς μολπή, Αἰολίδες χορδαί, Αἰολίδων πνοαὶ αὐλῶν, Æolian song, Æolian strings, the breath of Æolian flutes.

The subject and simile, as usual with Pindar, are united. The various sources of poetry, which gives life and lustre to all it touches, are here described; its quiet majestic progress enriching every subject (otherwise dry and barren) with a pomp of diction and luxuriant harmony of numbers; and its more rapid and irresistible course, when swoln and hurried away by the conflict of tumultuous passions. —[Gray.]

l. 3. *Helicon.* A romantic range of mountains in Boeotia, the gorges of which were sacred to Apollo and the Muses. Cf. Matthew Arnold, Empedocles on Etna :—

'Not here, O Apollo,
Are haunts meet for thee,
But where Helicon breaks down
In cliff to the sea.'

The 'harmonious springs' which took their progress from Helicon were Hippocrene and Aganippe.

l. 5. *laughing flowers.* A Latinism. Virgil, in the fourth eclogue, speaks of the *laughing* acanthus.

100   THE PROGRESS OF POESY.

ll. 7-12. Dr. Johnson has brought a characteristic objection against this passage. He says: 'Gray seems in his rapture to confound the images of *spreading sound* and *running water*. A *stream of musick* may be allowed; but where does *Musick*, however *smooth and strong*, after having visited the *verdant vales, rowl down the steep amain*, so as that *rocks and nodding groves rebellow to the roar*? If this be said of *Musick*, it is nonsense; if it be said of *Water*, it is nothing to the purpose.' Gray may, however, easily be defended. Johnson had forgotten, doubtless, that this very image is taken from Pindar, and that Gray had placed himself under the protection of Pindar. His exact meaning no doubt is, that poetry in early Greece was either of a smooth and majestic simplicity, like that of the gnomic poets, or of a brisk and laughing vivacity, like that of the lyrists, or else of a thundering music, as of emotion broken on the rocks of life, in the works of the tragic dramatists. Such imagery as this, however, is hardly to be paraphrased in detail.

l. 9. *Ceres' golden reign*, i.e. corn-fields. Demeter, the Ceres of the Romans, presided over the labours and the fruits of agriculture, and was represented in art garlanded with ears of corn.

l. 13. Power of harmony to calm the turbulent sallies of the soul. The thoughts are borrowed from the first Pythian of Pindar. —[Gray.]

The antistrophe opens with a direct address to the Lyre, which is kept up to the close of the epode. It is addressed as *shell*, because the great lyre of Apollo, the phorminx, was originally made of the hollow shell of a large tortoise, over which strings of sinew or catgut were drawn, and played upon with an ivory plectrum.

l. 17. *On Thracia's hills the Lord of War*. It was supposed that Thrace was the home of Ares, the god of war, no doubt on account of the ferocity of the mountain tribes of that country.

The allusion in ll. 17-19 seems to be to Orpheus, who is supposed to have lived in Thrace, and to have occupied himself, after the Argonautic expedition, with attempting to civilise his wild fellow-countrymen.

l. 20. This is a weak imitation of some incomparable lines in the same Ode.—[Gray.] *Perching*, i.e. as he perches; that is to say, the magic of the Lyre lulls the eagle of Zeus while he perches on his master's sceptred hand. It would seem, however, that the eagle would naturally choose the other hand to perch on.

NOTES.

l. 22. *flagging wing.* Horace Walpole says that this phrase was suggested to Gray by the famous Boccapadugli Eagle, a sculpture then considered to be an original Greek antique. But the expression is common to many poets earlier than Gray.

l. 25. Power of harmony to produce all the graces of motion in the body.—[Gray.]

l. 26. *warbled lay.* Warbling is commonly used for the soft singing of birds alone. According to Prof. Skeat the original meaning of the word is to twirl or whirl about, and no doubt it was given to the singing of birds from the motion which they make in song. But it is not inappropriately used here to express the soft, continuous, and vibrant sounds of the lyre, to which the voice and dance are attempered and harmonised.

l. 27. *Idalia.* This is one of the names of Venus, who had a temple at Idalion, in Cyprus. Gray appears, however, to take *Idalia* itself to be the name of a place sacred to the goddess.

Velvet-green. Johnson attacked Gray for inventing this epithet, which he says 'has something of cant. An epithet or metaphor drawn from Nature enobles Art; an epithet or metaphor drawn from Art degrades Nature.' The criticism is just, on the whole. But Gray had not invented the epithet, which is found in Milton, Pope, and elsewhere, while he may also be defended on the ground of the resemblance of well-grown and carefully-mown greensward to the pile of velvet.

l. 29. *Cytherea,* i.e. Venus, who was worshipped in the rocky island of Cythéra, off the coast of Laconia. It was said that here she first landed, when she rose from the foam of the sea.

l. 30. *antic,* here an adjective, meaning 'quaint' and 'sportive.' Cf. Dryden, The Medal, I:—
'Of all our *antic* sights and pageantry.'

l. 35. Μαρμαρυγὰs θηεῖτο ποδῶν· θαύμαζε δὲ θυμῷ.
Hom. Od. Θ. [ver. 265].—[Gray.]

l. 41. Λάμπει δ' ἐπὶ πορφυρέῃσι
Παρείῃσι φῶς ἔρωτος.
Phrynicus apud Athenæum.—[Gray.]

l. 42. To compensate the real and imaginary ills of life, the Muse was given to mankind by the same Providence that sends the Day, by its chearful presence, to dispel the gloom and terrors of the night.—[Gray.]

THE PROGRESS OF POESY.

l. 51. 'Or seen the Morning's well-appointed Star
Come marching up the eastern hills afar.'
Cowley.—[Gray.]
The couplet from Cowley has been wrongly quoted by Gray, and so continued by his different editors.—[Mit.] But Mitford himself misquotes it. The lines are these, and they form ll. 55–57 of Cowley's eighth Pindarique Ode, entitled Brutus:—
'One would have thought 't had heard the Morning crow,
Or seen her well-appointed Star
Come marching up the Eastern Hill afar.'

l. 53. *Hyperion's march.* Shakespeare preceded and Keats followed Gray in this false quantity. The accent should be on the third syllable, Hyperion, as Akenside, in the Hymn to the Naiads, l. 46:—
'When the might
Of *Hyperion*, from his noontide throne,
Unbends their languid pinions.'
Hyperion, so well known from Keats's magnificent romance, was ruler of the Sun during the reign of the Titans. He was the son of Uranus and Ge.

l. 54. Extensive influence of poetic Genius over the remotest and most uncivilised nations: its connection with liberty, and the virtues that naturally attend on it. [See the Erse, Norwegian, and Welsh fragments, the Lapland and American songs.]—[Gray.]
'Extra anni solisque vias.'—Virgil. [Æn. vi. 795.] 'Tutta lontana dal camin del sole.'—Petr. Canzon. 2.—[Gray.]
solar road. This is an Italianism, for which Gray excuses himself by the above reference to Petrarch. Pope had used the expression *solar walk* (Essay on Man, i. 102), and Dryden also. The allusion in ll. 54–58 is to the wealth of Icelandic poetry, which Gray seems to have been the first person in these islands to appreciate.

l. 66. Progress of Poetry from Greece to Italy, and from Italy to England. Chaucer was not unacquainted with the writings of Dante or of Petrarch. The Earl of Surrey and Sir Tho. Wyatt had travelled in Italy, and formed their taste there; Spenser imitated the Italian writers; Milton improved on them: but this School expired soon after the Restoration, and a new one arose on the French model, which has subsisted ever since.—[Gray.]
Delphi's steep. At Delphi there existed the oracular chasm on the side of Mount Parnassus over which the tripod was slung

upon which the Pythian Prophetess sat to breathe the mephitic exhalation that rose from the fountain of Cassotis. The little neighbouring town was a main seat of the cultus of Apollo.

l. 68. Ilissus was the river upon which Athens was built. Mœander, the modern Mendereh, was a famous stream of Asia Minor.

l. 73. *Where each old poetic mountain*, etc. Many years before, Gray had expressed his enthusiasm for the Alps in words which closely resemble these. In writing to West, on the 16th of November 1739, he says: 'In our little journey up to the Grande Chartreuse I do not remember to have gone ten paces without an exclamation which there was no restraining; not a precipice, not a torrent, not a cliff, but is pregnant with religion and poetry.'

l. 77. *Till the sad Nine*, etc., i.e. until the nine Muses, in the shape of poetry, ceased to flourish in the decline of Greece, and found a new harbour in Rome and the Latin genius.

l. 84. 'Nature's darling.'—Shakespeare.—[Gray.]

ll. 95-102. This antistrophe, the first portion of which is dedicated to Milton, contains adaptations of many of that poet's expressions, and in particular of that fine phrase from Paradise Lost, iii. 380:—

'Dark with excess of bright thy skirts appear.'
Milton [P. L. vi. 771].—[Gray.]

l. 98. 'Flammantia mœnia mundi.'—Lucret. [i. 74].—[Gray.]

l. 99. 'For the spirit of the living creature was in the wheels. And above the firmament that was over their heads, was the likeness of a throne, as the appearance of a saphire stone. This was the appearance of the glory of the Lord.'—Ezek. i. 20, 26, 28.—[Gray.]

l. 102. 'Οφθαλμῶν μὲν ἄμερσε· δίδου δ' ἡδεῖαν ἀοιδήν.
Hom. Od. [Θ. ver. 64].—[Gray.]

l. 105. Meant to express the stately march and sounding energy of Dryden's rhimes.—[Gray.]

l. 106. 'Hast thou clothed his neck with thunder?'—Job.—[Gray.]

l. 110. 'Words, that weep, and tears, that speak,'
Cowley.—[Gray.]

Gray here quotes incorrectly from memory. The line is the twentieth in The Prophet, in The Mistresse, 1647, and runs thus:—

'Tears which shall understand and speak.'

l. 111. We have had in our language no other odes of the sublime kind, than that of Dryden on St. Cecilia's Day; for Cowley (who

had his merit) yet wanted judgment, style, and harmony, for such a task. That of Pope is not worthy of so great a man. Mr. Mason indeed of late days has touched the true chords, and with a masterly hand, in some of his Choruses,—above all in the last of Caractacus:
'Hark! heard ye not yon footstep dread?' etc.—[Gray.]
l. 112. *what daring Spirit*, i. e. that of Gray himself.
l. 115. Διὸς πρὸς ὄρνιχα θεῖον, Olymp. ii. [159.] Pindar compares himself to that bird, and his enemies to ravens that croak and clamour in vain below, while it pursues its flight, regardless of their noise.—[Gray.]
l. 118. *before his infant eyes*. Dugald Stewart has remarked in connection with this line :—'Gray, in describing the infantine reveries of poetical genius, has fixed with exquisite judgment on that class of our conceptions which are derived from *visible* objects.' (Philosophy of the Human Mind.) It is, moreover, a little touch of autobiography on the part of the poet, and in connection with the lines that follow, may be compared with the confidences of the Epitaph to the Elegy in a Country Churchyard. Both the one and the other are a little too self-conscious in their simplicity.

THE BARD.

The Bard was begun in December 1754, immediately upon the completion of The Progress of Poesy. The exordium was finished in March 1755; Gray nicknamed it 'Odikle,' and worked upon it fitfully until the autumn of 1755, when he laid it aside. He had begun it at Peterhouse; he took it up again at Pembroke in May 1757, being freshly inspired by a concert given by John Parry, the famous blind harper, and then finished it promptly. It was published, together with The Progress of Poesy, in the Odes of 1757, where it bore the title of Ode II. The text of 1757, which is given here, agrees in the most minute particulars with that of 1768; but the notes, though all by Gray, differ, and are here dated. Both editions are preceded by this Advertisement,—'The following Ode is founded on a Tradition current in Wales, that EDWARD THE FIRST, when he compleated the conquest of that country, ordered all the Bards, that fell into his hands, to be put to death.'
l. 1. *ruthless King*. Edward I, who subdued Wales in 1282.

l. 4. 'Mocking the air with colours idly spread.'
Shakespeare's King John [Act v. Sc. 1].—[Gray. 1768.]
l. 5. The Hauberk was a texture of steel ringlets, or rings interwoven, forming a coat of mail, that sat close to the body, and adapted itself to every motion.—[Gray. 1768.]
l. 9. 'The crested adder's pride.'
Dryden, Indian Queen.—[Gray. 1768.]
l. 11. *Snowdon* was a name given by the Saxons to that mountainous tract which the Welch themselves call *Craigian-eryri:* it included all the highlands of Caernarvonshire and Merionethshire, as far east as the river Conway. R. Hygden, speaking of the castle of Conway built by King Edward the first, says, 'Ad ortum amnis Conway ad clivum montis Erery;' and Matthew of Westminster (ad ann. 1283), 'Apud Aberconway ad pedes montis Snowdoniæ fecit erigi castrum forte.'—[Gray. 1768.]
shaggy side = rough with woods seen in profile against the sky. Cf. Keats, Ode to Psyche, 54, 5 :—
'Far, far around shall those dark-clustered trees
Fledge the wild-ridgèd mountains steep by steep;'
and Milton's Lycidas, 54 :—
'Nor on the *shaggy* top of Mona high.'
l. 13. Gilbert de Clare, surnamed the Red, Earl of Gloucester and Hertford, son-in-law to King Edward.—[Gray. 1768.]
l. 14. Edmond de Mortimer, Lord of Wigmore. They both were *Lords-Marchers*, whose lands lay on the borders of Wales, and probably accompanied the king in this expedition.—[Gray. 1768.]
couch'd = laid his spear in rest, ready for the attack.
l. 19. The image was taken from a well-known picture of Raphaël, representing the Supreme Being in the vision of Ezekiel. There are two of these paintings (both believed original), one at Florence, the other [in the Duke of Orleans' collection] at Paris.—[Gray. 1768.]
l. 20. *stream'd like a meteor.* This is a mere adaptation of Milton, Paradise Lost, i. 535 :—
'Shone, like a meteor, streaming to the wind.'
Dryden describes the same phenomenon in three vigorous lines :—
'The seeming Stars fall headlong from the skies,
And shooting through the Darkness gild the Night
With sweeping Glories and long Trails of Light.'
l. 27. *Vocal no more*, i. e. with echoes.. The sense of *vocal* here is

not the primary one of 'pertaining to the voice,' but 'endowed with a voice,' namely, the voice of echo, reverberating the sorrows of the Lyre.

l. 28. *Hoel*, son of Owen Gwynedd, Prince of North Wales, a famous general and bard. *Llewellyn*, the Welsh prince who fell before Edward I in the fastnesses of Snowdon; some of his poems have been preserved. *Cadwallo* and *Urien*, bards of whose productions nothing remains; 'brave Urien,' it appears, had slept upon his craggy bed for upwards of seven hundred years at the supposed date of this poem. Gray seems to have made a mistake in speaking of *Modred*, or else he invented the name. He got his information from Dr. Evans' Dissertatio de Bardis.

l. 35. The shores of Caernarvonshire opposite to the isle of Anglesey.—[Gray. 1768.]

l. 38. Cambden and others observe, that eagles used annually to build their aerie among the rocks of Snowdon, which from thence (as some think) were named by the Welch *Craigian-eryri*, or the crags of the eagles. At this day (I am told) the highest point of Snowdon is called *the eagle's nest*. That bird is certainly no stranger to this island, as the Scots, and the people of Cumberland, Westmoreland, etc., can testify: it even has built its nest in the Peak of Derbyshire. [Gray. 1768.]

l. 40. 'As dear to me as are the ruddy drops
That visit my sad heart.'
Jul. Cæsar [Act ii. Sc. 1].—[Gray. 1768.]

l. 47. See the Norwegian ode [The Fatal Sisters] that follows.—[Gray. 1768.]

l. 49. *Weave the warp*. In weaving, the threads which are stretched lengthwise in the loom are called the *warp*, from *weorpan* to cast, because they are thrown over by the shuttle; those which cross them at right angles are called the *woof* or weft. The proper form of the second term is *oof*. Cf. Skeat, *passim*.

l. 51. Dr. Johnson considered this the weakest line in Gray's poems.

l. 52. *characters*, i. e. the letters. Cf. Sylvester's translation of Du Bartas:—

'The World's a Book in Folio, printed all
With God's great Works in letters Capitall;
Each Creature is a Page; and each Effect
A fair *character*, void of all defect.'

NOTES. 107

l. 53. *Mark the year, and mark the night*, i.e. Sept. 21, 1327, when Edward II was murdered in Berkeley Castle by Gournay and Ogle.

l. 56. Edward the Second, cruelly butchered in Berkley Castle.— [Gray. 1768.]

l. 57. Isabel of France, Edward the Second's adulterous Queen.— [Gray. 1768.]

l. 60. Triumphs of Edward the Third in France.—[Gray. 1768.]

l. 64. Death of that King, abandoned by his Children, and even robbed in his last moments by his Courtiers and his Mistress.— [Gray. 1768.]

l. 66. *obsequies* = funeral ceremonies, from the Latin *obsequiæ*, rites following upon decease.

l. 67. Edward, the Black Prince, dead some time before his Father. —[Gray. 1768.]

l. 71. Magnificence of Richard the Second's reign. See Froissard and other contemporary writers.—[Gray. 1768.]

l. 77. Richard the Second (as we are told by Archbishop Scroop [and the confederate Lords in their manifesto], by Thomas of Walsingham, and all the older Writers)' was starved to death. The story of his assassination by Sir Piers of Exon, is of much later date. —[Gray. 1757.]

l. 83. Ruinous wars of York and Lancaster.—[Gray. 1768.]

l. 87. Henry the Sixth, George Duke of Clarence, Edward the Fifth, Richard Duke of York, etc., believed to be murthered secretly in the Tower of London. The oldest part of that structure is vulgarly attributed to Julius Cæsar.—[Gray. 1768.]

l. 89. Margaret of Anjou, a woman of heroic spirit, who struggled hard to save her Husband and her Crown.—[Gray. 1768.]

Henry the Fifth.—[Gray. 1768.]

l. 90. Henry the Sixth very near being canonised. The line of Lancaster had no right of inheritance to the Crown.—[Gray. 1768.]

l. 91. The white and red roses, devices of York and Lancaster.— [Gray. 1768.]

l. 93. *the bristled Boar*. Cf. Otway's Orphan :—
'The Tyrant of the Woods
With all his dreadful Bristles raised up high.'
The silver Boar was the badge of Richard the Third ; whence he was usually known in his own time by the name of *the Boar*.— [Gray. 1768.]

THE BARD.

l. 94. *the thorny shade*, i. e. the shade of the thorny branches of the rose-trees.

l. 99. Eleanor of Castile died a few years after the conquest of Wales. The heroic proof she gave of her affection for her Lord is well known. The monuments of his regret and sorrow for the loss of her, are still to be seen at Northampton, Geddington, Waltham, and other places.—[Gray. 1757.]

ll. 109, 110. Gray originally closed this strophe with the lines :—
'From Cambria's thousand hills a thousand strains
Triumphant tell aloud, another *Arthur* reigns.'
He cancelled this, as not expressing his meaning, which was to indicate the genuine Welsh descent of the Tudor kings.

It was the common belief of the Welch nation, that King Arthur was still alive in Fairy-Land, and should return again to reign over Britain.—[Gray. 1768.]

l. 110. Accession of the Line of Tudor.—[Gray. 1757.] Both Merlin and Taliessin had prophesied, that the Welch should regain their sovereignty over this island; which seemed to be accomplished in the House of Tudor.—[Gray. 1768.]

l. 113. Mr. Leslie Stephen has observed that nothing but the absence of a comma prevents the 'gorgeous Dames' from sharing 'bearded Majesty' with the 'Statesmen old.' This is a strange slip for Gray to have made ; he did not reflect that readers less precise than himself would ruin his effect by a careless punctuation.

l. 115. *a Form.* Queen Elizabeth.

l. 117. Speed, relating an audience given by Queen Elizabeth to Paul Dzialinski, ambassador of Poland, says: 'And thus she, lion-like rising, daunted the malapert Orator no less with her stately port and majestical deporture, than with the tartnesse of her princelie checkes.'—[Gray. 1768.]

l. 119. *symphonious* = harmonious. A Miltonic word :—
'The sounds *symphonious* of ten thousand harps.'

l. 121. Taliessin, Chief of the Bards, flourished in the VIth Century. His works are still preserved, and his memory held in high veneration among his Countrymen.—[Gray. 1757.]

l. 123. *soaring as she sings.* This famous phrase appears to be an improvement upon a line of Congreve's Ode to the Earl of Godolphin, l. 56 :—
'And soars with rapture while she sings.'

l. 126. 'Fierce wars and faithful loves shall moralise my song.'
Spenser, Proëme to the Fairy Queen.—[Gray. 1768.]
l. 127. *fairy*, here used, as an adjective, in the somewhat strained sense of 'romantic.'
l. 128. *buskin'd measures*, i.e. dramatic verse, poetry that wears the buskin, or conventional stocking of the actor. It is here used to denote the Tragedies of Shakespeare.
l. 131. *the Cherub-Choir*. Gray is here thinking of Milton's angelic music, perhaps mainly of the sublime lines in At a solemn Music, 6-13:—
'That undisturbed song of pure content,
Aye sung before the sapphire-colour'd throne
To him who sits thereon;
With saintly shout, and solemn jubilee,
Where the bright seraphim in burning row
Their loud up-lifted angel trumpets blow;
And *the cherubic host in thousand quires*
Touch their immortal harps of golden wires.'
l. 133. The succession of Poets after Milton's time.—[Gray. 1768.]

THE FATAL SISTERS.

The Fatal Sisters, according to a note to the original MS. at Pembroke College, was written in 1761. It was first published, as here reprinted, in the edition of 1768. It is a paraphrase of an Icelandic court-poem of the eleventh century, entitled Darradar Liod or the Lay of Darts. According to Vigfusson and Powell, it refers to the battle of Clontarf, fought on Good Friday, 1014, and represents the Weird Sisters as appearing before the battle, and weaving the web of the fate of Ireland and of King Brian. See Corpus Poeticum Boreale, i. 281-283, for the Icelandic text.

l. 1. The Valkyriur were female Divinities, servants of Odin (or Woden), in the Gothic mythology. Their name signifies Chusers of the slain. They were mounted on swift horses, with drawn swords in their hands; and in the throng of battle selected such as were destined to slaughter, and conducted them to Valkalla, the hall of Odin, or paradise of the Brave; where they attended the banquet, and served the departed Heroes with horns of mead and ale.—[Gray.]

l. 2. *the loom of Hell*. The Valkyries are supposed to be singing, as they prepare for battle. The original is very loosely paraphrased

THE DESCENT OF ODIN.

by Gray. 'The weird sisters appear before the Battle of King Brian weaving the web of Ireland's fate.' Vigfusson and Powell.

l. 3. 'How quick they wheel'd, and, flying, behind them shot Sharp sleet of arrowy show'r.'
                                Milton's Par. Regained [iii. 324].—[Gray.]
l. 4. 'The noise of battle hurtled in the air.'
                                Shakesp. Jul. Cæsar [Act. ii. Sc. 2].—[Gray.]
l. 8. *Orkney's woe*. The death of Sigurd of Orkney, son of Brian. *Randver's bane* = 'Randvéss bana' in the original; the meaning is obscure.

l. 11. *the weights*, i.e. those which keep the web in its place.

l. 17. The names of the Sisters, in the original, are Hilda, Hiorthrimol, Sangrida, and Swipol.

l. 25. *Weave the crimson web of war*. In the Icelandic poem this refrain occurs at the beginning of three successive staves:—
                 'Vindom, vindom vef darraðar'
(let us wind, let us wind the web of darts).

l. 31. *Geira*. The real name is Gunna, and Gray seems to have known this, for that name occurs on his first draft of the poem, now in Pembroke College.

l. 32. *the youthful King*. It is not known who this young king was.

ll. 37–40. This is equivalent to saying that the nation or tribe which has hitherto been confined to the sea-coast, shall, in consequence of this victory, rule over the interior as well, i.e. the Norsemen shall penetrate into the rich province of Ireland.

l. 41. *the dauntless Earl* = Brian. *a king* = Brian's son, Sigurd.

l. 45. *Eirin*. In the Icelandic, 'Írar,' i.e. the Irish. Gray has misunderstood the sympathy of the Valkyries, which is against and not for the woes of Eirin.

l. 59. *Scotland*. There is nothing about Scotland in the Icelandic poem.

l. 62. *faulchion* or falchion, a broad short sword, curved towards the point.

THE DESCENT OF ODIN.

The Descent of Odin, written at Cambridge in 1761, first appeared in the volume of 1768. It is a paraphrase of the ancient Icelandic lay called Vegtams kvida, and sometimes Baldrs draumar. The best edition of the original is that given in the Corpus Poeticum Boreale, vol. i. p. 181, under the heading 'Balder's Doom.' Gray has omitted to translate the first four lines. This is a much more ancient poem than the preceding, and is attributed by Vigfusson and Powell to the Ballad Poet, the author of Thrymskvida.

l. 1. *the King of Men.* The god Odin or Woden.

l. 2. *his coal-black steed.* Odin's horse, Sleipni.

l. 4. Niflheimr, the hell of the Gothic nations, consisted of nine worlds, to which were devoted all such as died of sickness, old age, or by any other means than in battle. Over it presided Hela, the Goddess of Death.—[Gray.]

l. 18. *the moss-grown pile.* The barrow of the 'prophetic maid,' Sibyl or Volva.

l. 22. *the runic rhyme.* There is nothing about runes in this poem, but Gray had read elsewhere that there were certain runic characters which, when they were written down, had power to rouse the dead.

l. 24. The original word is Valgalldr; from Valr 'mortuus,' and Galldr 'incantatio.'—[Gray.]

l. 37. *A Traveller.* Odin calls himself Vegtam, or Way-wise, that he may not have to tell his real name to Volva; he adds that he is the son of Valtam, War-wise.

ll. 41, 42. These lines are thus rendered by Vigfusson and Powell: —'For whom are the benches strewn with mail-coats, and the hall so fairly hung with painted shields?'

l. 44. *The pure beverage of the bee* = mead, the favourite drink of the Norsemen, brewed for Balder, the Sun-god, the son of Odin, whose death, though almost an immortal, Volva now proceeds to prophesy.

l. 55. Hoder, the blind god, shot an arrow made of mistletoe, which was the only thing on earth which had not sworn to spare Balder, and the shaft, guided by Loki, the evil genius of the Æsir, entered Balder's body and killed him. Cf. Matthew Arnold, 'Balder Dead,' ll. 1-8 :—

> 'So on the floor lay Balder dead : and round
> Lay thickly strewn swords, axes, darts, and spears,
> Which all the Gods in sport had idly thrown
> At Balder, whom no weapon pierced or clove;
> But in his breast stood fixt the fatal bough
> Of mistletoe, which Lok the Accuser gave
> To Hoder, and unwitting Hoder threw—
> 'Gainst that alone had Balder's life no charm.'

THE TRIUMPHS OF OWEN.

l. 65. *A wond'rous Boy*. Wali, who should neither wash his hands nor comb his hair till he had borne the murderer of Balder to the funeral fire. Cf. Vigfusson and Powell.

l. 90. *Lok* is the evil Being, who continues in chains till the Twilight of the Gods approaches: when he shall break his bonds; the human race, the stars, and sun, shall disappear; the earth sink in the seas, and fire consume the skies: even Odin himself and his kindred-deities shall perish. For a further explanation of this mythology, see Mallet's Introduction to the History of Denmark, 1755, quarto.—[Gray.]

THE TRIUMPHS OF OWEN.

Of the Triumphs of Owen no MS. is known to exist in Gray's handwriting. It was probably composed in 1764. It was published in the volume of 1768, with this Advertisement by Gray:— 'Owen succeeded his Father Griffin in the Principality of North-Wales, A.D. 1120. This battle was fought near forty Years afterwards.' Gray, who did not know Welsh, paraphrased this fragment from Evan's Specimens of the Welsh Poetry, 1764, where it was given in a prose version. The original was the composition of Gwalchmai the son of Melir, and the battle to which it refers was fought in 1157.

l. 1. Owen succeeded his father Griffith app Cynam, as Prince of North Wales, in 1137.

l. 4. North-Wales.—[Gray.]

l. 14. *Lochlin*, Denmark.—[Gray.]

l. 20. The red Dragon is the device of Cadwallader, which all his descendants bore on their banners.—[Gray.]

l. 25. *Talymalfra*. Tal Moelvre.

l. 27. This and the three following lines are not in the former editions, but are now added from the author's MS.—[Mason.]

l. 31. From this line, to the conclusion, the translation is indebted to the genius of Gray, very little of it being in the original, which closes with a sentiment omitted by the translator: 'And the glory of our Prince's wide-wasting sword shall be celebrated in a hundred languages, to give him his merited praise.'—[Mason.]

ELEGY WRITTEN IN A COUNTRY CHURCH-YARD.

The Elegy written in a Country Church-Yard was begun at Stoke Poges in the autumn of 1742, probably on the occasion of the funeral of Jonathan Rogers, on the 31st of October. In the winter of 1749 Gray took it in hand again, at Cambridge, after the death of his aunt, Mary Antrobus. He finished it at Stoke on the 12th of June 1750. The poem was circulated in MS., and on the 10th of February 1751 Gray received a letter from the editor of the Magazine of Magazines, asking leave to publish it. The poet refused, and wrote next day to Horace Walpole, directing him to bring it out in pamphlet form. Accordingly, so soon as the 16th of February, there appeared anonymously 'An Elegy wrote in a Country Church Yard. London: Printed for R. Dodsley in Pall-Mall; and sold by M. Cooper in Pater-Noster Row. 1751. (Price sixpence.)' There was a preface by Horace Walpole. The text here given is that of the Edition of 1768, which appears to be authoritative and final. Gray has appended the following bibliographical note to the Pembroke MS.:—'Published in Febry. 1751, by Dodsley, & went thro' four editions, in two months; and afterwards a fifth, 6th, 7th, & 8th, 9th, 10th, & 11th; printed also in 1753 with Mr. Bentley's Designs, of wch. there is a 2d edition; & again by Dodsley in his Miscellany, vol. iv., & in a Scotch Collection call'd the Union; translated into Latin by Chr. Anstey, Esq., and the Revd. Mr. Roberts, & published in 1762, & again in the same year by Rob. Lloyd, M.A.' Besides these legitimate editions, the poem was largely pirated; the Magazine of Magazines printed it on the last of February, the London Magazine on the last of March, and the Grand Magazine of Magazines on the last of April. It first appeared with Gray's name as the last of the Six Poems of 1753.

l. 1. *Curfew.* Gray's own spelling is *curfeu.* The bell rung at night-fall to warn the inhabitants to extinguish their fires, from the French *couvre-feu,* cover-fire. Chaucer speaks of 'abouten courfew-time.' The word had become almost obsolete, when Gray revived it by using it in this popular poem. Dr. Warton, in his Notes on Pope, suggests that there is a grammatical difficulty in this line, and proposes to read

'The curfew tolls!—the knell of parting day.'

This difficulty seems to be that *to toll* is an intransitive verb, but this is incorrect. Hood says—

'They went and told the sexton,
And the sexton *tolled the bell.*'
and Dryden, Prologue to Troilus and Cressida, 1679, ll. 20, 21:—
'For humour farce, for love thy rhyme dispense,
That *tolls the knell* for their departed sense.'
'... squilla di lontano
Che paia 'l giorno pianger, che si muore.'
Dante, Purgat. l. 8.—[Gray.]

l. 2. *herd* is a plural noun of number. In almost all modern editions of Gray the verb is misprinted *winds*.

l. 5. *glimmering* = faintly and dimly lighted, with twinkling points of illumination. This word has been much misused by modern foppery. In a recent copy of verses by a recognised hand I read :—

'All is a-grey, and the sky's in a *glimmer*,
A *glimmer* as ever a sky should be.'

Cf. Skeat for the relations of the word to 'gleam,' 'glitter,' and 'glimpse.'

l. 7. *the beetle* = the Cock-Chafer (Melolontha vulgaris), sometimes called the Maybug, that with loud and blundering flight assaults the twilight traveller.

l. 8. *And drowsy tinklings lull the distant folds.* Cf. Matthew Arnold, Lines written in Kensington Gardens, l. 8 :—
'How thick the tremulous sheep-cries come.'

l. 10. *The mopeing owl* = moping, that is to say, dull and melancholy. The *ignavus bubo* of Ovid.

l. 13. *Beneath those rugged elms, etc.* This is the stanza which bears most certainly the stamp of Stoke Poges Churchyard.

l. 14. *Where heaves the turf.* Cf. Parnell, A Night-Piece on Death, ll. 29, 30 (1722) :—
'Those Graves with bending Osier bound,
That nameless heave the crumbled Ground.'

l. 16. *rude* = uncultured, rustically simple.

l. 19. *The cock's shrill clarion.* Cf. Dryden, The Cock and the Fox, ll. 43-46 (1700) :—
'More certain was the crowing of a Cock
To number Hours, than is an Abbey-Clock;
And sooner than the Mattin-Bell was rung,
He clap'd his Wings upon his Roost, and sung.'

l. 21. A resemblance has here been detected to a line in Thomson's Seasons, Winter, 311, 2:—
'In vain for him the officious wife prepares
The fire fair-blazing.'
l. 22. *ply* = be busily engaged upon.
l. 23. *to lisp their sire's return.* It is a licence to make the verb to lisp transitive. Gray means to hail their sire's return in lisping accents.

l. 33. Gray has, in this stanza, done little more than paraphrase one by his friend Richard West:—
'Ah me! what boots us all our boasted power,
Our golden treasure, and our purple state;
They cannot ward the inevitable hour,
Nor stay the fearful violence of fate.'

l. 39. *the long-drawn isle.* More properly spelt *aisle*. *fretted vault.* Cf. Hamlet, ii. 2:—
'This majestic roof *fretted* with golden fire.'
There can be no doubt that the services at King's College Chapel, Cambridge, inspired this couplet. *fretted* is, properly, adorned with fillets interlaced at right angles; it is here used to express the effect of any compound architectural ornament.

l. 40. *The pealing anthem.* Milton had said in Il Penseroso, 163:—
'There let the pealing organ blow,
To the full-voiced quire below,
In service high, and *anthem* clear.'

l. 41. All this portion of the Elegy recalls Parnell's beautiful poem A Night Piece, to which reference has already been made. Parnell had said:—
'The Marble Tombs that rise on high,
Whose Dead in vaulted Arches lye,
Whose Pillars swell with sculptur'd Stones,
Arms, Angels, Epitaphs and Bones,
These (all the poor Remains of State)
Adorn the *Rich*, or praise the *Great*;
Who, while on Earth in Fame they live,
Are senseless of the Fame they give.'

l. 41. *storied* = bearing an inscription or a written history. Milton, in Il Penseroso, had spoken of *storied* windows. *animated bust* = a portrait in bronze or marble so vivid that the personage seems to breathe anew in it, the *spirantia aera* of Virgil.

l. 43. *provoke*. A Latinism, used, not in the sense of to annoy, to rouse to anger, but to call forth, the Latin *provocare*.

l. 47. *rod of empire*. Gray originally wrote 'reins of empire,' but altered the phrase on recollection that Tickell had used it in his lines to the Earl of Warwick.

l. 48. *the living lyre*. This is copied from Cowley, who in his ode called The Resurrection, l. 13, says :—
  'Begin the Song, and strike the *living lyre*.'
Pope recollected this line, when, in Windsor Forest, he attributed a *living Harp* to Cowley.

l. 51. *rage* = fervour, enthusiasm. Cf. Lee's Mithridates :—
  'at Delphos, when the glorious Fury
  Kindles the Blood of the prophetick Maid.'
This meaning of the word came in with the classical revolution in poetic taste.

l. 53. The origin of these famous lines has been traced to a passage in the Contemplations of Bishop Hall : 'There is many a rich stone laid up in the bowells of the earth, many a *fair pearle in the bosome of the sea*, that never was seene, nor never will be.' The second couplet of the stanza has been supposed, very needlessly, to be a reminiscence of two lines in the Pharonnida of Chamberlayne, 1659 :—
  'Like beauteous flowers which vainly waste their scent
  Of odors in unhaunted deserts.'

l. 57. John Hampden, the Buckinghamshire patriot and cousin of Oliver Cromwell, was one of the first and ablest opponents of the tax of ship-money.

l. 58. *little Tyrant*. It has been remarked that most artists, in illustrating this poem, have absurdly taken the *little tyrant* to be a child. *Little* here means 'puny, insignificant,' little in comparison with a great tyrant, such as Charles I.

l. 60. Prof. Hales remarks that 'the prejudice against Cromwell was extremely strong throughout the eighteenth century, even among the more liberal-minded. That cloud of 'detractions rude,' of which Milton speaks in his noble sonnet to our 'chief of men' as in his own day enveloping the great republican leader, still lay thick and heavy over him. His wise statesmanship, his unceasing earnestness, his high-minded purpose, were not yet seen.' It may be added that Waller had seen these things, and had been reprimanded for seeing them.

l. 65. *circumscrib'd*, a prosaic and unwieldy word, which nothing but habit prevents from disturbing our sense of the melody of this passage. *growing virtues*, i. e. their virtues which were ready to grow, had not this bound prevented.

l. 72. After this verse, in the Mason MS. of the poem, are the four following stanzas :—

> 'The thoughtless World to Majesty may bow,
> Exalt the brave, and idolize Success;
> But more to Innocence their Safety owe
> Than Pow'r and Genius e'er conspir'd to bless.
>
> And thou, who mindful of th' unhonour'd Dead,
> Dost in these Notes their artless Tale relate,
> By Night and lonely Contemplation led
> To linger in the gloomy Walks of Fate :
>
> Hark! how the sacred Calm, that broods around,
> Bids ev'ry fierce tumultuous Passion cease;
> In still small Accents whisp'ring from the Ground,
> A grateful Earnest of eternal Peace.
>
> No more, with Reason and thyself at Strife,
> Give anxious Cares and endless Wishes room;
> But thro' the cool sequester'd Vale of Life
> Pursue the silent Tenour of thy Doom.'

l. 75. *sequestered* = 'secluded, withdrawn.' Cf. Joseph Beaumont's Psyche, xx. 265 :—
'Thus from exterior Troubles *sequestered*.'

l. 76. *tenour* = 'course, direction.'

l. 77. *these bones* = the bones of such as these.

l. 78. *still erected nigh* = still standing, in spite of its frail and temporary character.

l. 84. There is perhaps a reminiscence here of the celebrated couplet in Tickell's Elegy on Addison :—
'There taught us how to live; and (oh! too high
The price for knowledge) *taught us how to die*.'

l. 85. This stanza has been considered very difficult to construe.

118 ELEGY WRITTEN IN A COUNTRY CHURCH-YARD.

The meaning, however, may perhaps be this:—The poet, moralising on the universal desire of mankind to be individually remembered after death, asks, who was ever such a prey to dumb forgetfulness, to stupid thoughtlessness, as to resign the pleasant anxiety of life, and leave the warm precincts of day, without casting a thought back to the past, and hoping to be remembered in the future. The necessity of being loved and recollected is carried on into the succeeding stanza. On the other hand, it may be that 'dumb forgetfulness' is the Lethe of death, *Lethaea silentia*, as it is translated by Mr. H. A. J. Munro. It is to be observed that the poetical fire which sustained the earlier part of the poem on so high a level, is now beginning visibly to flag.

l. 92. Petrarch, Son. 169.—[Gray.]

l. 93. *For thee, etc.*
'If chance that e'er somé pensive spirit more
  By sympathetic musings here delayed,
  With vain tho' kind enquiry shall explore,
  Thy once loved haunt, this long deserted shade.'—
                                                    Mason MS.

l. 95. *If chance* = if it should chance.

l. 99. Cf. Milton, Arcades, 50:—
'And from the boughs brush off the evil dew.'

l. 100. *upland*. The proper meaning of this adjective is merely rural, of the country, as distinguished from of the town; but the sense here is that which is now usual, namely, belonging to the higher slopes, to land in its topmost undulations.

'On the high brow of yonder hanging lawn.'—Mason MS.
Here, in the Mason MS., follows this stanza:—
'Him have we seen the Greenwood Side along,
  While o'er the Heath we hied, our Labours done,
  Oft as the Woodlark piped her farewell Song,
  With whistful eyes pursue the setting sun.'

l. 102. Luke compares this with a line from Spenser's Ruines of Rome, 28:—
'Showing her *wreathed rootes* and naked armes.'

l. 107. *woeful-wan* = pale with dejection. Mitford desired that these two adjectives should be freed from the handcuffs of the hyphen.

l. 108. *hopeless love* = i.e. love which has no hope of success.
l. 109. *custom'd hill*. Customed is a very unusual word, though to be found in Shakespeare;—
  'No common wind, no *customèd* event,'
and in Sylvester:—
  'Pale, swoln as Toad (though *customèd* to vaunt).'
It means 'usual, customary.'
l. 115. The 'hoary-headed swain' himself being uneducated, and unable to read.
l. 116. *grav'd* = engraved.
Gray originally inserted at this place a very beautiful stanza, which was printed in some of the first editions, but afterwards omitted, Mason says, because Gray thought that it formed too long a parenthesis. He continued, however, to vacillate between discarding and retaining it, and it can hardly be regarded as cancelled:—
  'There scatter'd oft, the earliest of y° Year,
    By Hands unseen are Showers of vi'lets found;
  The Redbreast loves to build and warble there,
    And little Footsteps lightly print the Ground.'
l. 117. *the lap of Earth*. Cf. Milton, Paradise Lost, x. 777:—
  'How glad would lay me down,
    As in my mother's lap,'
and Spenser, Faery Queen, v. 7, 9:—
  'For other beds the Priests there used none,
    But on their mother Earth's deare Lap did lie.'
Mitford quotes from Pliny, Hist. Nat. ii. 63, 'Nam terra novissime complexa *gremio* jam a reliqua natura abnegatos, tum maxime, *ut mater*, operit.'
l. 126. *draw* is not an imperative. The construction is:—Do not seek to disclose his merits or to draw his frailties, etc. There is a stranger form of speech in the parenthesis of the next line. It is difficult to see by what figure a man's merits and his frailties can be said to repose on the bosom of God.
l. 127. '... paventosa speme.'—Petrarch, Son. 114.—[Gray.]

A LONG STORY.

My authority for the text of A Long Story is Gray's original MS. at Pembroke College. The piece was only printed once in Gray's lifetime, when it formed the fourth of the Six Poems in 1753, and was illustrated by a view of Stoke Manor, interpreted by Bentley from a rough sketch by Gray, which is still in existence, bound up with Bentley's drawings. The poem, as stated by Gray himself in the Pembroke MS., was written in August 1750, in consequence of the incident that a Lady Schaub and Lady Cobham's niece, Miss Speed, paid the poet an afternoon call, and found him abroad. Gray declined to reprint A Long Story in 1768, on the ground that it was so personal as to have become unintelligible.

l. 2. *An ancient pile.* The mansion at Stoke Poges, in Buckinghamshire, originally inhabited by Sir Edward Coke, and afterwards by the Earls of Huntingdon and the family of Hatton. Of this beautiful specimen of Tudor architecture, which was built in 1555, nothing remains but the fantastic chimneys, and a rough shed, which is used as a stable. It was pulled down in 1789, at the instance of Wyatt, and was replaced by a heavy Georgian manor-house on a different site. The ruin was fitted up as a studio for Sir Edwin Landseer, and he was working in it when he became deranged in 1852. When Gray came to Stoke in 1742, the Manor House was inhabited by the ranger of Windsor Forest, Viscount Cobham, who died in 1749. His widow was the heroine of the present poem.

l. 6. *achievements.* In heraldry, the armorial escutcheon fixed in a church or hall after the death of a noble personage. The modern form is 'hatchment.'

l. 9. *spatious* = spacious. A return to the Latin derivative of the word *spatiosus*.

l. 11. [Sir Christopher] Hatton, prefer'd by Queen Elizabeth for his graceful Person and fine Dancing.—[Gray.]

the Brawls. A kind of stately dance, a corruption of the French *bransle.* Skeat, quoting Cotgrave, says 'a *brawle* or daunce, where, in many men and women, holding by the hands, sometimes in a ring, and otherwhiles at length, move all together.' Cf. Shakespeare, Love's Labour's Lost, iii. 9, 'a French *brawl*,' and Sir John Davies' Orchestra (1596), st. 62, l. 4:—

'Whereof a thousand *brawles* he doth compound.'

l. 12. *The Seal.* The Great Seal, used in sealing writs to summon parliament, and carried before Sir Christopher Hatton, as lord chancellor. *Maces.* Silver staves borne in front of persons in authority.

l. 23. *buff.* Leather, generally light yellow in colour, of which rough military uniforms were made. Sometimes the uniform itself was called *buff*, as in this instance.

l. 25. *cap-a-pee*, more frequently 'cap-à-pie'; from head to foot. The modern French form is 'de pied en cap.'

l. 28. *her art of killing*. In the artificial language of gallantry, charming ladies were understood to *kill* their male admirers by the sudden action of their charms. This warrior 'from France' was a Lady Schaub, who undertook to call on Gray. The 'other Amazon' was Miss Harriet Speed, Lady Cobham's niece and companion.

l. 37. *capucine* or 'capuchin,' an outer garment for women, made with a hood, like that of a Capuchin monk of the order of St. Francis.

l. 41. *Mr. Purt*. Mason tells us that this personage was much displeased at the liberty Gray had taken in introducing his name. Robert Purt, a Fellow of King's College, Cambridge, was at that time living at Stoke Poges. He died in 1752.

l. 51. The laws against vagabonds were very severe. Mitford quotes a *commission* of Henry IV against this species of *vermin*.

l. 53. This is a humorous account of the call which Lady Schaub and Miss Speed ventured to pay the poet, at Lady Cobham's request.

l. 64. *tester* = the square canopy over a four-post bedstead.

l. 66. *embroglio* or 'imbroglio,' an intricate and confused condition of things. A striking resemblance has been pointed out between this and the succeeding stanzas and some lines in Prior's story of The Dove, particularly in this stanza from the latter piece:—

'Her keys he takes, her door unlocks,
Thro' wardrobe, and thro' closet bounces,
Peeps into every chest and box,
Turns all her furbelows and flounces.'

l. 71. *hoops*. The crinoline worn by ladies in the eighteenth century. In Bentley's drawing to this poem the Muses are seen in the act of this process of concealment.

l. 79. *whisk*. It is the imperative form of the verb. 'They flew out of the window [as if they had received the command] Whisk!'

l. 80. *a spell*, viz. the note Lady Schaub left regretting that Mr. Gray was not at home.

l. 85. *the Apparatus*. This word properly means a collection of objects brought together for a certain purpose, and is so used here.

122   THE INSTALLATION ODE.

l. 103. *Styack*, the House-Keeper.—[Gray.]
l. 112. *the People of condition* = the quality, all the gentlefolks present.
l. 116. The Steward.—[Gray.]
l. 120. A famous Highwayman hang'd the week before.—[Gray.]
l. 129. *hagged face* = the face of a *hag* or ugly old woman or witch. Skeat says that the more familiar 'haggard' is a corruption of this word.

THE INSTALLATION ODE.

The Installation Ode was the latest of Gray's poems. He offered to write it on the occasion of the installation of Augustus-Henry Fitzroy, Duke of Grafton, as Chancellor of the University. He began it at the close of 1748, and in April 1749 it was finished. For three months, Dr. J. Randall of King's, the music professor in the University, waited regularly on Gray with the score. Dr. Burney was much disappointed at not being asked to set the poem. It was performed in the Senate-House on the occasion for which it was written, and was published anonymously at the expense of the University in quarto form:—'Ode performed in the Senate-House at Cambridge, July 1, 1769, at the Installation of Augustus-Henry Fitzroy, Duke of Grafton, Chancellor of the University. Cambridge, 1769.'

l. 1. *avaunt* = begone! From the French 'en avant,' go on! Norton Nicholls relates : ' One morning when I went to Mr. Gray as usual after breakfast, I knocked at his door, which he threw open, and exclaimed with a loud voice,—
           'Hence, avaunt! 'tis holy ground!'
I was so astonished, that I almost feared he was out of his senses; but this was the beginning of the Ode which he had just composed.' Cf. Virgil, Æneid, vi. 258 :—
           'Procul, o procul este profani.'
l. 7. *consecrated bowers*. G. Wakefield points out the similarity to A Midsummer Night's Dream, iii. 2 :—
           ' Near to her close and *consecrated bower*.'
l. 27. Mason observes that this stanza, which is supposed to be sung by Milton, is very judiciously composed in the stanza of the Ode on the Nativity. Milton and Newton are selected as Cambridge men of surpassing eminence.

NOTES.   123

l. 29. *Camus* = the river Cam or Granta.

l. 31. Cf. Thomson's Spring :—
'In long excursion skims the *level lawn*.'

l. 39. Edward III, the founder of Trinity College, Cambridge, added the fleur de lys to the arms of England. Hallam has given high commendation to the mode in which this procession of Cambridge worthies is conducted.

l. 41. Mary de Valentia, Countess of Pembroke, daughter of Guy de Chatillon, Comte de St. Paul in France; of whom tradition says that her husband, Audemar de Valentia, Earl of Pembroke, was slain at a tournament on the day of his nuptials. She was the foundress of Pembroke College or Hall, under the name of Aula Mariæ de Valentia.—[Gray.]

l. 42. Elizabeth de Burg, Countess of Clare, was wife of John de Burg, son and heir of the Earl of Ulster, and daughter of Gilbert de Clare, Earl of Gloucester, by Joan of Acres, daughter of Edward the First. Hence the poet gives her the epithet of *princely*. She founded Clare Hall.—[Gray.]

l. 43. Margaret of Anjou, wife of Henry the Sixth, foundress of Queen's College.

Elizabeth Widville, wife of Edward the Fourth, hence called the paler rose, as being of the house of York. She added to the foundation of Margaret of Anjou.—[Gray.]

l. 45. Henry the Sixth and Eighth. The former the founder of King's, the latter the greatest benefactor to Trinity College.— [Gray.]

l. 64. Gray seems here to have made use of a rejected stanza of his own, written originally for the Elegy in a Country Churchyard :—
' Hark how the sacred calm that broods around
Bids every fierce tumultuous passion cease;
In still small accents whisp'ring from the ground
A grateful earnest of eternal peace.'

l. 66. Countess of Richmond and Derby; the mother of Henry the Seventh, foundress of St. John's and Christ's Colleges.—[Gray.]

l. 70. The Countess was a Beaufort, and married to a Tudor: hence the application of this line to the Duke of Grafton, who claims descent from both these families.—[Gray.]

l. 71. *judging eye*. This expression is repeatedly made use of by Pope.

124   SONNET.

l. 83. *thy youthful brow.* The Duke of Grafton was thirty-four years of age.
l. 84. Lord Treasurer Burleigh was Chancellor of the University in the reign of Queen Elizabeth.—[Gray.]
l. 93. This fulsome reference to the reigning House has been stigmatised as the only ridiculous passage in all Gray's works. It was, no doubt, a matter of obligation that he should make some such compliment, and his awkwardness in doing it may reconcile us to the fact that he had refused the office of poet-laureate.

SONNET.

This sonnet was written at Stoke in August, 1742. Richard West, whose friendship with Gray in early life has been described in the Introduction, died on the 1st of June, 1742, and was buried at Hatfield. An impassioned address to his memory occurs in the Latin fragment of Gray's, in hexameters, called De Principiis Cogitandi.

l. 1. Wordsworth has made a celebrated attack on the diction of this sonnet in the Preface to the second edition of his Lyrical Ballads (1800), pp. xxiv, xxv. He says:—
'I will here adduce a short composition of Gray, who was at the head of those who by their reasonings have attempted to widen the space of separation betwixt Prose and Metrical composition, and was more than any other man curiously elaborate in the structure of his own poetic diction.' He then quotes Gray's sonnet. 'It will easily be perceived that the only part of this sonnet which is of any value is [lines 6, 7, 8, 13, 14]: it is equally obvious that except in the rhyme, and in the use of the single word "fruitless" for fruitlessly, which is so far a defect, the language of these lines does in no respect differ from that of prose.' Wordsworth's opinion bears great weight, but in this instance the expression of it seems slightly disingenuous. It has been pointed out that 'if we allow the sun to be called "Phœbus," and if we pardon the "green attire," there is not a single expression in the sonnet which is fantastic or pompous.

l. 3. *Descant,* i. e. a tune with various modulations. Cf. Milton:—
'The wakeful nightingale;
She all night long her amorous *descant* sung.'
l. 8. Rogers points out that Dryden, in his translation of Ovid, says:—

'And in my ear the imperfect accent dies.'
l. 14. Colley Cibber had said, in his stage version of Richard III, ii. 2:—
'So we must weep, because we weep in vain.'
Cf. also Charles Fitzgeoffrey's Sir Francis Drake (1596), p. 103:—
'O therefore doe we plaine,
And therefore weepe, because we weepe in vaine.'

HYMN TO IGNORANCE.

Written in December, 1742, immediately after Gray's return to Peterhouse, Cambridge.

l. 1. Gray was extremely dissatisfied with Cambridge at this part of his career. He found it intellectually arid, socially stagnant. He says, in a letter to Dr. Wharton, on the 27th December, 1742: 'As to Cambridge, it is as it was for all the world; and the people are as they were; that is half-ill, half-well; I wish with all my heart they were all better, but what can one do?'

Hail, horrors, hail! Cf. Milton, Paradise Lost, i. 205:—
'Hail, horrors, hail!'
l. 3. *rushy* = lined with rushes. Cf. Tennyson:—
'Or dimple in the dark of *rushy* coves.'
l. 4. A flagrant Miltonism. Cf. Paradise Lost, vii. 310:—
'Where rivers now
Stream, and *perpetual draw their humid train.*'
l. 11. That is to say, 'three years have passed since I was last in Cambridge.' This would give us the date of the fragment, if Gray's memory had not erred. It was four years, since the winter of 1738.

l. 14. *ægis*, the breastplate of metal scales worn by Pallas Athena, on the centre of which was fixed the head of Medusa which turned every one who looked at it to stone.

l. 37. *Sesostris.* The Greek name of the Egyptian conqueror Rhamses III, of the nineteenth dynasty, who is said to have ruled Ethiopia, Asia, and Thrace. John Philips has a similar passage in his Blenheim (Works, 1720):—

'As erst *Sesostris* (proud Ægyptian King)
That *Monarchs harness'd* to his Chariot yok'd.'

STANZAS TO MR. RICHARD BENTLEY.

These beautiful lines were written in 1752 as a compliment to Bentley for drawing the designs for the *Six Poems* of 1753. Unfortunately the sole existing MS. had the corner of the last stanza torn off when Mason found it. It seems to me unnecessary to give Mason's or Mitford's conjectural restoration, or to venture on one myself.

l. 3. There is a certain resemblance here to the strophe in Dryden's Ode to the Memory of Mrs. Anne Killigrew, in which the lady's efforts in painting are described :—
'And all the large domains which the dumb *Sister* swayed.'
ll. 7, 8. The construction is:—'See each dream, wrought in fancy's airy colouring, awake to local symmetry and life.'
l. 17. I thought at one time that *one* was a misprint for *me*; but I suppose that there is no error, and that the meaning is that in this degenerate age that diviner inspiration is not given to any *one*.
l. 21. This is written on the supposition that the brilliant colourlessness of the diamond is the result of the combination of the colours of all other jewels, by which they neutralise one another in hue, and form a general treasury of light.

ODE ON VICISSITUDE.

Mason states that he heard Gray say that the *Épitre à ma Sœur* of the French poet J. B. L. Gresset (1709-1777) gave him the first idea of this ode, which was found after his death in a pocket-book of the year 1754. Mason printed it, as it has until now been reprinted, restored, and completed by himself in his gaudy style. It is here given from a copy of Gray's MS. made by Stonehewer, and preserved at Pembroke College.

ll. 2, 4. *dew-bespangled wing.* Luke quotes from the Hippolytus of Seneca, i. 11 :—
'Rorifera mulcens aura,
Zephyrus vernas evocat herbas.'
l. 3. *vermeil* = of a clear rosy red, the colour of vermilion. A word almost confined to the poets.
ll. 9, 10. No doubt a reminiscence of Lucretius, i. 260 :—

'Hinc nova proles,
Artubus infirmis teneras lasciva per herbas
Ludit.'

l. 25-28. Cf. Shelley's To a Sky-lark :—
'With thy clear keen joyance
Languor cannot be:
Shadow of annoyance
Never came near thee:
Thou lovest; but ne'er knew love's sad satiety.
We look before and after,
And pine for what is not.'

l. 34. The construction is 'Hope gilds deepest shades.'

l. 42. *sabler tints of woe.* Sables were black mourning garments, from the fur of the sable, which is usually yellowish-brown, but in the best sorts a full black. As an adjective the word is used, almost exclusively by the poets, for a tint of funeral black. Sylvester says, in his Bethulin's Rescue, iv. 313, 314:—
'Still, therefore, cover'd with a sable Shrowd,
Hath Shee kept home, as all to sorrow vow'd.'

l. 45. This is the stanza in which Gray approaches most closely to Gresset. But the resemblance to various well-known passages of Wordsworth is still more obvious. It is not possible but that the latter poet owed to Gray the suggestion of his:—
'To me the meanest flower that blows can give
Thoughts that do often lie too deep for tears.'

l. 55. *chrystalline.* There is no excuse for this redundant *h*; the word is derived from κρύσταλλος, 'ice.' The accentuation should be 'crýstalline,' as in Shakespeare and Shelley, but Milton says crystàlline, as Gray does here.

EPITAPH ON MRS. JANE CLERKE.

This lady was the wife of Dr. John Clerke, an early college friend of Gray's, and afterwards a physician at Epsom. She died in child-birth, April 27, 1757, and was buried in the church of Beckenham, Kent.

l. 1. *the silent marble weeps.* Cf. Pope's Epitaph on Edmund Duke of Buckingham (1735):—
'This weeping marble had not ask'd thy Tear.'

Epitaph on a Child.

This sextain, which was first printed in 1884, was written in June 1758, at the request of Dr. Thomas Wharton, whose then only son had died in infancy early in the month of April.

Sketch of his own Character.

l. 1. *importune* = to solicit favours earnestly and urgently.

l. 5. It is possible that the scramble for patronage which Gray witnessed at the coronation of George III in September of this year inspired this line of self-gratulation. Goldsmith is supposed to have taken these verses as the model for his character of Burke in Retaliation.

l. 6. *Squire*. At that time Fellow of St. John's College, Cambridge, and afterwards Bishop of St. David's. Dr. S. Squire died in 1766. Bishop Warburton one day met Dean Tucker, who said that he hoped his Lordship liked his situation at Gloucester, on which the sarcastic Bishop replied, that never bishoprick was so *bedeaned*, for that his predecessor Dr. Squire had made *religion his trade*, and that he (Dr. Tucker) had made *trade his religion*.

Epitaph on Sir William Williams.

Sir William Peere Williams, Bart., a young soldier whose 'fine Vandyck head' Gray admired, was killed at the storming of Belleisle, June 13, 1761. He was in a dejected frame of mind, and, inadvertently walking too close to the enemy's sentinels, was shot through the body. Frederick Montague induced Gray to write the Epitaph, which was to have been inscribed on a monument at Belleisle. Walpole describes Williams as 'a gallant and ambitious young man, who had devoted himself to war and politics.' In the expedition to Aix he was on board the 'Magnanime' with Lord Howe, and was deputed to receive the capitulation.

l. 3. This line is directly imitated from one in Sophocles. The sense is 'Each (= every) Muse adorned his mind, each Grace adorned his frame.'

l. 5. *his voluntary sword*. This phrase is copied by Sir Walter Scott in Marmion:—

'Since riding side by side, our hand
First draw the *voluntary brand*.'

l. 10. *Belleisle*. A fortified island off the coast of Morbihan, captured by the English forces in the summer of 1761.

WELSH FRAGMENTS.

These fragments probably belong to the year 1764, and were inspired, like The Triumphs of Owen, by Evans's Specimens of Welch Poetry. The Gododin is a heroic poem, attributed to the Bard Aneurin, and celebrating the Battle of Cattraeth, in the sixth century.

l. 3. *Deïra.* The province of Maxima Caesariensis, now the West Riding of Yorkshire.

l. 11. *Cattraeth,* or Katraeth, probably between Galashiels and Kelso.

l. 25. *tusky boar* = furnished with tusks. The more legitimate form is 'tusked.'

l. 36. *shiver'd* = shattered into splinters, as by lightning.

IMPROMPTU.

In June 1766, after Gray had been spending two months with 'Reverend Billy,' the Rev. William Robinson, at his rectory of Denton, in Kent, these verses were found in a drawer of the room he had occupied. The house was that built for Henry Fox, the first Lord Holland (1705-1774), in imitation of Cicero's Formian villa at Baiæ, by Lord Newborough.

l. 17. *Bute.* The famous prime minister, John Stuart, Third Earl of Bute (1713-1792).

l. 18. In another draft, Gray wrote the names of 'Shelburne, Rigby, Calcraft.'

AMATORY LINES.

These lines are thought to be a paraphrase of an epigram in the sixth book of the Erotikon of Hercules Strozius the Elder, 'Ad Carolum.' Nothing is known of the circumstances under which Gray wrote them, but the original MS. was in the possession of the Countess de Viry (Miss Speed), who presented it, with the ensuing song, to the Rev. Thomas Leman, when he visited her in Switzerland. Leman handed the verses to Warton, who printed them in his edition of Pope.

SONG.

This song was written at the request of Miss Speed, to an old air of Geminiani (1680-1762)—the thought adapted from the French.

K

FROM PROPERTIUS.

This is the finest of Gray's paraphrases from the antique, being not a school-exercise, but a poem from his mature period. It was not known until in 1884 it was first printed from the poet's MS. in Pembroke College.

l. 3. *Cynthia*. The Latin elegiac poet Propertius (B.C. 51?-13?) celebrated in his pieces the incidents of his passion for a woman whom he named *Cynthia*, whose real name appears to have been Hostia. She is not mentioned by Propertius in the particular passage Gray is translating, but he introduces her name to enlighten the English reader, who is ignorant of the context.

l. 6. *Rhime*. This paraphrase is an excellent example of Gray's peculiarities in spelling. At this time (1742) he preserved the orthography of a much older age, the age of Dryden, and, in particular, gave capital letters to all his nouns, although most writers had long ceased to do this. Dryden had spelt the word *rhyme* 'Rime.' Cf. To the Memory of Mr. Oldham, l. 21 :—

'But mellows what we write to the dull sweets' of Rime,'
and Skeat points out instances in the 1623 folio Shakespeare. The form 'rhime' is used by Oldham himself, in his Satyr on Poetry (1682) l. 62 :—

'A man of Parts, of Rhiming, and Renown.'
But the word is usually spelt 'rhyme,' 'in which case,' as Skeat remarks, 'it is one of the worst spelt words in the language. This ridiculous spelling was probably due to confusion with the Greek word "rhythm," and it is, I believe, utterly impossible to find an instance of the spelling "rhyme" before A.D. 1550.'

l. 9. *Coan web*. At Cos, one of the Sporades, were fabricated the semi-transparent textures known as 'Coae vestes.' Propertius' words are :—

'Sive togis illam fulgentem incedere Cois,
Hoc totum e Coa veste volumen erit;'

'if she comes forward shining in Coan garments, it is enough to produce from me a whole volume on the Coan manufacture of tissues,' an amusing instance of that pedantry which is characteristic of Propertius, but which does not prevent him from being one of the most emotional writers of antiquity.

l. 29. *you'll see*. The address is to Mæcenas.

NOTES. 131

l. 30. A very happy eighteenth-century rendering of
'Maxima de nihilo nascitur historia.'

ll. 35, 36. What Propertius says is, 'I should not sing of the Titans, nor of Pelion placed upon Ossa, and Ossa upon Olympus.'

l. 38. *the Persian.* Xerxes.

·l 39. This refers to the expeditions of Marius against the Cimbri in the beginning of the century towards the close of which the poet wrote.

l. 43. *Mutina* = Modena, where Antony besieged Decimus Brutus after the death of Cæsar, until the town was relieved by the forces of Augustus under Hirtius and Pansa.

l. 44. *the ensanguined Wave of Sicily.* This is a reference to the capture of Sicily by Sextus Pompeius Magnus, and to the defeat of his navy off Naulochus, probably a recent event when the poem was written.

l. 45. *scepter'd Alexandria.* The capture of Pharos by Augustus. What Propertius says is:—
'Ptolemæeæ litora capta Phari.'

l. 49. *And hoary Nile.* The Romans were in the habit of adorning their triumphal pageants with figures of the towns and rivers of the conquered peoples.

l. 55. *Callimachus.* The famous African poet of the third century B.C., of whose elegies but a few fragments remain to us. He was imitated by the Latin elegiac writers, and particularly by Propertius.

l. 56. *Phlegra's blasted Plain.* The Phlegræi Campi, the volcanic flats extending from Capua to Cumæ. Propertius means that the horrors of this region demand a more masculine pen than that of the Alexandrian Callimachus.

l. 65. Gray has quite missed the meaning here. What Propertius says is that it is glorious to die for love, but that there is also a happiness in life spent in the infatuation of an unalterable love for one single object. The turn of the original is very delicate and pathetic:—
'laus altera, si datur uno
Posse frui: fruar o solus amore meo!'

ll. 69, 70. Cf. Dryden's Cleomenes, ii. 2:—
'My ravished eyes behold such charms about her,
I can die with her, but not live without her.'

l. 81. *Machaon.* The son of Æsculapius, and like him a physician. He cured the sore in the foot of the *Melian* Philoctetes.

FROM DANTE.—NOTES.

l. 83. *Phœnix*, the son of Amyntor, King of the Dolopes. His father put out his eyes, but his sight was restored to him by Chiron, the Centaur.

l. 100. *the short Marble* = 'in exiguo marmore.' Cf. Pope, Epitaph on Elijah Fenton, l. 1:—

'This modest Stone, what few *vain Marbles* can.'

FROM DANTE.

This translation from Dante was first printed in 1884, from a MS. in the handwriting of Mitford in the possession of Lord Houghton. It is worthy of close study; the vigour of the diction, the harmony and originality of the versification, and the concentrated tragic passion of these lines raise them, although a translation, to a level with Gray's most considerable contributions to literature. They may be compared with Mr. H. A. J. Munro's noble Latin version ot the same episode. From the spelling, I take it to have been written about 1742.

l. 1. *the griesly Fellon* = Count Ugolino della Gherardesca, a Pisan, whose crime was not proven; he was accused of having sold to Florence and Lucca certain lands of Pisa.

l. 2. *clotter'd* = clotted.

l. 5. *nathless* = nevertheless. The Anglo-Saxon form is *ná the læs* (no- th- less.)

l. 13. *Ruggieri* or Roger degli Ubaldini, the traitorous Archbishop of Pisa, through whose wicked fraud Ugolino, with two sons and two grandsons, had been starved to death.

l. 29. *Pisa's Mount.* Monte San Giuliano, which rises between Pisa and Lucca.

l. 32. *Lanfranc there.* Gualandi, Sismondi, and Lanfranchi, three Ghibelline auxiliaries of the Archbishop.

l. 55. *my little dear Anselmo* = 'Anselmuccio mio.'

l. 60. *mought* = might, an archaic form, the preterite of the Old English 'mowe,' to be able. It still survives in some country dialects. Gray uses it to give an ancient air to his narrative.

THE END.

December, 1885.

The Clarendon Press, Oxford,
LIST OF SCHOOL BOOKS,
PUBLISHED FOR THE UNIVERSITY BY

HENRY FROWDE,

AT THE OXFORD UNIVERSITY PRESS WAREHOUSE,
AMEN CORNER, LONDON.

*** *All Books are bound in Cloth, unless otherwise described.*

LATIN.

Allen. *An Elementary Latin Grammar.* By J. BARROW ALLEN, M.A. *Forty-second Thousand* . . . . . . Extra fcap. 8vo. 2s. 6d.

Allen. *Rudimenta Latina.* By the same Author. Extra fcap. 8vo. 2s.

Allen. *A First Latin Exercise Book.* By the same Author. *Fourth Edition.* . . . . Extra fcap. 8vo. 2s. 6d.

Allen. *A Second Latin Exercise Book.* By the same Author.
Extra fcap. 8vo. 3s. 6d.

Jerram. *Anglice Reddenda; or, Easy Extracts, Latin and Greek, for Unseen Translation.* By C. S. JERRAM, M.A. *Fourth Edition.*
Extra fcap. 8vo. 2s. 6d.

Jerram. *Reddenda Minora; or, Easy Passages, Latin and Greek, for Unseen Translation.* For the use of Lower Forms. Composed and selected by C. S. JERRAM, M.A. . . . . . Extra fcap. 8vo. 1s. 6d.

Lee-Warner. *Hints and Helps for Latin Elegiacs.*
Extra fcap. 8vo. 3s. 6d.

Lewis and Short. *A Latin Dictionary*, founded on Andrews' Edition of Freund's Latin Dictionary. By CHARLTON T. LEWIS, Ph.D., and CHARLES SHORT, LL.D. . . . . 4to. 25s.

Nunns. *First Latin Reader.* By T. J. NUNNS, M.A. *Third Edition.*
Extra fcap. 8vo. 2s.

Papillon. *A Manual of Comparative Philology* as applied to the Illustration of Greek and Latin Inflections. By T. L. PAPILLON, M.A. *Third Edition.*
Crown 8vo. 6s.

Ramsay. *Exercises in Latin Prose Composition.* With Introduction, Notes, and Passages of graduated difficulty for Translation into Latin. By G. G. RAMSAY, M.A., Professor of Humanity, Glasgow. *Second Edition.*
Extra fcap. 8vo. 4s. 6d.

Sargent. *Passages for Translation into Latin.* By J. Y. SARGENT, M.A. . . . . Extra fcap. 8vo. 2s. 6d.

Caesar. *The Commentaries* (for Schools). With Notes and Maps. By CHARLES E. MOBERLY, M.A.
Part I. *The Gallic War. Second Edition.* . . Extra fcap. 8vo. 4s. 6d.
Part II. *The Civil War.* . . . . . . Extra fcap. 8vo. 3s. 6d.
The Civil War. Book I. *Second Edition.* . . Extra fcap. 8vo. 2s.

Catulli Veronensis *Carmina Selecta,* secundum recognitionem ROBINSON ELLIS, A M. . . . . Extra fcap. 8vo. 3s. 6d.

Cicero. *Selection of interesting and descriptive passages.* With Notes. By HENRY WALFORD, M.A. In three Parts. *Third Edition.*
Extra fcap. 8vo. 4s. 6d.
Part I. *Anecdotes from Grecian and Roman History.* . limp, 1s. 6d.
Part II. *Omens and Dreams; Beauties of Nature.* . . limp, 1s. 6d.
Part III. *Rome's Rule of her Provinces.* . . . . limp, 1s. 6d.

Cicero. *Pro Cluentio.* With Introduction and Notes. By W. RAMSAY, M.A. Edited by G. G. RAMSAY, M.A. *Second Edition.* Extra fcap. 8vo. 3s. 6d.

Cicero. *Selected Letters* (for Schools). With Notes. By the late C. E. PRICHARD, M.A., and E. R. BERNARD, M.A. *Second Edition.*
Extra fcap. 8vo. 3s.

Cicero. *Select Orations* (for Schools). *First Action against Verres; Oration concerning the command of Gnaeus Pompeius; Oration on behalf of Archias; Ninth Philippic Oration.* With Introduction and Notes. By J. R. KING, M.A. *Second Edition.* . . . . Extra fcap. 8vo. 2s. 6d.

Cicero. *Philippic Orations.* With Notes, &c. by J. R. KING, M.A. *Second Edition.* . . . . 8vo. 10s. 6d.

Cicero. *Select Letters.* With English Introductions, Notes, and Appendices. By ALBERT WATSON, M.A. *Third Edition.* . . . 8vo. 18s.

Cornelius Nepos. With Notes. By OSCAR BROWNING, M.A. *Second Edition.* . . . . . . Extra fcap. 8vo. 2s. 6d.

Horace. With a Commentary. Volume I. *The Odes, Carmen Seculare,* and *Epodes.* By EDWARD C. WICKHAM, M.A., Head Master of Wellington College. *Second Edition.* . . . Extra fcap. 8vo. 5s. 6d.

Livy. *Selections* (for Schools). With Notes and Maps. By H. LEE-WARNER, M.A. . . . . Extra fcap. 8vo.
Part I. *The Caudine Disaster.* . . . . . . limp, 1s. 6d.
Part II. *Hannibal's Campaign in Italy.* . . . . limp, 1s. 6d.
Part III. *The Macedonian War.* . . . . . . limp, 1s. 6d.

Livy. *Book I.* With Introduction, Historical Examination, and Notes. By J. R. SEELEY, M.A. *Second Edition.* . . . . . 8vo. 6s.

Livy. *Books V—VII.* With Introduction and Notes. By A. R. CLUER, B.A. . . . . Extra fcap. 8vo. 3s. 6d.

LIST OF SCHOOL BOOKS. 3

Livy. *Books XXI—XXIII.* With Introduction and Notes. By
M. T. TATHAM, M.A. . . . . . Extra fcap. 8vo. *Nearly ready.*

Ovid. *Selections* (for the use of Schools). With Introductions and
Notes, and an Appendix on the Roman Calendar. By W. RAMSAY, M.A.
Edited by G. G. RAMSAY, M.A. *Second Edition.* . Extra fcap. 8vo. 5s. 6d.

Ovid. *Tristia*, Book I. Edited by S. G. OWEN, B.A.
Extra fcap. 8vo. 3s. 6d.

Persius. *The Satires.* With Translation and Commentary by
J. CONINGTON, M.A., edited by H. NETTLESHIP, M.A. *Second Edition.*
8vo. 7s. 6d.

Plautus. *The Trinummus.* With Notes and Introductions. By C. E.
FREEMAN, M.A., Assistant Master of Westminster, and A. SLOMAN, M.A., Master
of the Queen's Scholars of Westminster. . . . Extra fcap. 8vo. 3s.

Pliny. *Selected Letters* (for Schools). With Notes. By the late
C. E. PRICHARD, M.A., and E. R. BERNARD, M.A. *Second Edition.*
Extra fcap. 8vo. 3s.

Sallust. *Bellum Catilinarium* and *Jugurthinum*. With Introduction and Notes, by W. W. CAPES, M.A. . . . Extra fcap. 8vo. 4s. 6d.

Tacitus. *The Annals.* Books I—IV. Edited, with Introduction and
Notes for the use of Schools and Junior Students, by H. FURNEAUX, M.A.
Extra fcap. 8vo. 5s.

Terence. *Andria.* With Notes and Introductions. By C. E. FREEMAN,
M.A., and A. SLOMAN, M.A. . . . . . Extra fcap. 8vo. 3s.

Virgil. With Introduction and Notes, by T. L. PAPILLON, M.A.
In Two Volumes. . . . Crown 8vo. 10s. 6d.; Text separately, 4s. 6d.

GREEK.

Chandler. *The Elements of Greek Accentuation* (for Schools).
By H. W. CHANDLER, M.A. *Second Edition.* . Extra fcap. 8vo. 2s. 6d.

Liddell and Scott. *A Greek-English Lexicon,* by HENRY GEORGE
LIDDELL, D.D., and ROBERT SCOTT, D.D. *Seventh Edition.* . 4to. 36s.

Liddell and Scott. *A Greek-English Lexicon,* abridged from LIDDELL
and SCOTT's 4to. edition, chiefly for the use of Schools. *Twenty-first Edition.*
Square 12mo. 7s. 6d.

Veitch. *Greek Verbs, Irregular and Defective:* their forms, meaning,
and quantity; embracing all the Tenses used by Greek writers, with references
to the passages in which they are found. By W. VEITCH, LL.D. *Fourth Edition.*
Crown 8vo. 10s. 6d.

Wordsworth. *Graecae Grammaticae Rudimenta in usum Scholarum.*
Auctore CAROLO WORDSWORTH, D.C.L. *Nineteenth Edition.* . 12mo. 4s.

Wordsworth. *A Greek Primer, for the use of beginners in that
Language.* By the Right Rev. CHARLES WORDSWORTH, D.C.L., Bishop of
St. Andrew's. *Seventh Edition.* . . . . Extra fcap. 8vo. 1s. 6d.

Wright. *The Golden Treasury of Ancient Greek Poetry;* being a Collection of the finest passages in the Greek Classic Poets, with Introductory Notices and Notes. By R. S. WRIGHT, M.A. . . Extra fcap. 8vo. 8s. 6d.

Wright and Shadwell. *A Golden Treasury of Greek Prose;* being a Collection of the finest passages in the principal Greek Prose Writers, with Introductory Notices and Notes. By R. S. WRIGHT, M.A., and J. E. L. SHADWELL, M.A. . . . . Extra fcap. 8vo. 4s. 6d.

A SERIES OF GRADUATED READERS.—

First Greek Reader. By W. G. RUSHBROOKE, M.L., Second Classical Master at the City of London School. *Second Edition.*
Extra fcap. 8vo. 2s. 6d.

Second Greek Reader. By A. M. BELL, M.A.
Extra fcap. 8vo. 3s. 6d.

Third Greek Reader. In Preparation.

Fourth Greek Reader; being Specimens of Greek Dialects. With Introductions and Notes. By W. W. MERRY, M.A., Rector of Lincoln College. . . . . Extra fcap. 8vo. 4s. 6d.

Fifth Greek Reader. Selections from Greek Epic and Dramatic Poetry, with Introductions and Notes. By EVELYN ABBOTT, M.A.
Extra fcap. 8vo. 4s. 6d.

THE GREEK TESTAMENT.—

Evangelia Sacra Graece. . . . Fcap. 8vo. *limp*, 1s. 6d.

The Greek Testament, with the Readings adopted by the Revisers of the Authorised Version.
Fcap. 8vo. 4s. 6d.; or on writing paper, with wide margin, 15s.

Novum Testamentum Graece juxta Exemplar Millianum.
18mo. 2s. 6d.; or on writing paper, with large margin, 9s.

Novum Testamentum Graece. Accedunt parallela S. Scripturae loca, necnon vetus capitulorum notatio et canones Eusebii. Edidit CAROLUS LLOYD, S.T.P.R., necnon Episcopus Oxoniensis.
18mo. 3s.; or on writing paper, with large margin, 10s. 6d.

The New Testament in Greek and English. Edited by E. CARDWELL, D.D. . . . . 2 vols. crown 8vo. 6s.

Outlines of Textual Criticism applied to the New Testament. By C. E. HAMMOND, M.A. *Fourth Edition.* . . Extra fcap. 8vo. 3s. 6d.

Aeschylus. *Agamemnon.* With Introduction and Notes, by ARTHUR SIDGWICK, M.A. *Second Edition.* . . . . . Extra fcap. 8vo. 3s.

Aeschylus. *The Choephoroi.* With Introduction and Notes, by the same Editor. . . . . Extra fcap. 8vo. 3s.

Aeschylus. *Prometheus Bound.* With Introduction and Notes, by A. O. PRICKARD, M.A. *Second Edition.* . . . Extra fcap. 8vo. 2s.

LIST OF SCHOOL BOOKS.

Aristophanes. *The Clouds.* With Introduction and Notes, by W. W. MERRY, M.A. *Second Edition.* . . . . . Extra fcap. 8vo. 2s.

Aristophanes. *The Acharnians.* By the same Editor. *Second Edition.*
Extra fcap. 8vo. 2s.

Aristophanes. *The Frogs.* By the same Editor.
Extra fcap. 8vo. 2s.

Cebes. *Tabula.* With Introduction and Notes, by C. S. JERRAM, M.A.
Extra fcap. 8vo. 2s. 6d.

Demosthenes and Aeschines. *The Orations of Demosthenes and Æschines on the Crown.* With Introductory Essays and Notes. By G. A. SIMCOX, M.A., and W. H. SIMCOX, M.A. . . . . . . 8vo. 12s.

Euripides. *Alcestis.* By C. S. JERRAM, M.A. Extra fcap. 8vo. 2s. 6d.

Euripides. *Helena.* For Upper and Middle Forms. By the same Editor. . . . . Extra fcap. 8vo. 3s.

Euripides. *Iphigenia in Tauris.* With Introduction and Notes. By the same Editor. . . . . Extra fcap. 8vo. 3s.

Herodotus. *Selections,* edited, with Introduction, Notes, and a Map, by W. W. MERRY, M.A. . . . . . Extra fcap. 8vo. 2s. 6d.

Homer. *Iliad,* Books I-XII. With an Introduction, a brief Homeric Grammar, and Notes. By D. B. MONRO, M.A. Extra fcap. 8vo. 6s.

Homer. *Iliad,* Book I. By the same Editor. *Third Edition.*
Extra fcap. 8vo. 2s.

Homer. *Iliad,* Books VI and XXI. With Notes, &c. By HERBERT HAILSTONE, M.A. . . . . . . Extra fcap. 8vo. 1s. 6d. each.

Homer. *Odyssey,* Books I-XII. By W. W. MERRY, M.A. *Thirty-second Thousand.* . . . . . . Extra fcap. 8vo. 4s. 6d.

Homer. *Odyssey,* Books XIII-XXIV. By the same Editor. *Second Edition.* . . . . Extra fcap. 8vo. 5s.

Homer. *Odyssey,* Book II. By the same Editor. Extra fcap. 8vo. 1s. 6d.

Lucian. *Vera Historia.* By C. S. JERRAM, M.A. *Second Edition.*
Extra fcap. 8vo. 1s. 6d.

Plato. *The Apology.* With a revised Text and English Notes, and a Digest of Platonic Idioms, by JAMES RIDDELL, M.A. . . 8vo. 8s. 6d.

Plato. *Selections* (including the whole of the *Apology* and *Crito*). With Introductions and Notes by J. PURVES, M.A., and a Preface by B. JOWETT, M.A.
Extra fcap. 8vo. 6s. 6d.

Sophocles. In Single Plays, with English Notes, &c. By LEWIS CAMPBELL, M.A., Professor of Greek in the University of St. Andrew's, and EVELYN ABBOTT, M.A. . . . . . Extra fcap. 8vo. *limp.*

Oedipus Tyrannus, Philoctetes. New and Revised Edition, 2s. each.
Oedipus Coloneus, Antigone. 1s. 9d. each.
Ajax, Electra, Trachiniae. 2s. each.

6 CLARENDON PRESS

Sophocles. *Oedipus Rex:* Dindorf's Text, with Notes by W. BASIL
JONES, D.D., Lord Bishop of S. David's. . Extra fcap. 8vo. *limp*, 1s. 6d.

Theocritus. Edited, with Notes, by H. KYNASTON, D.D. (late
SNOW), Head Master of Cheltenham College. *Third Edition.*
Extra fcap. 8vo. 4s. 6d.

Xenophon. *Easy Selections* (for Junior Classes). With a Vocabulary,
Notes, and Map. By J. S. PHILLPOTTS, B.C.L., Head Master of Bedford
School, and C. S. JERRAM, M.A. *Third Edition.* . Extra fcap. 8vo. 3s. 6d.

Xenophon. *Selections* (for Schools). With Notes and Maps. By
J. S. PHILLPOTTS, B.C.L. *Fourth Edition.* . . Extra fcap. 8vo. 3s. 6d.

Xenophon. *Anabasis,* Book I. With Notes and Map. By J. MARSHALL,
M.A., Rector of the High School, Edinburgh. . . Extra fcap. 8vo. 2s. 6d.

Xenophon. *Anabasis,* Book II. With Notes and Map. By C. S.
JERRAM, M.A. . . . . Extra fcap. 8vo. 2s.

Xenophon. *Cyropaedia,* Books IV, V. With Introduction and Notes,
by C. BIGG, D.D. . . . . Extra fcap. 8vo. 2s. 6d.

ENGLISH.

Reading Books.

—— *A First Reading Book.* By MARIE EICHENS of Berlin; edited
by ANNE J. CLOUGH. . . . . . Extra fcap. 8vo. *stiff covers*, 4d.

—— *Oxford Reading Book,* Part I. For Little Children.
Extra fcap. 8vo. *stiff covers*, 6d.

—— *Oxford Reading Book,* Part II. For Junior Classes.
Extra fcap. 8vo. *stiff covers*, 6d.

Tancock. *An Elementary English Grammar and Exercise Book.*
By O. W. TANCOCK, M.A., Head Master of King Edward VI's School, Norwich.
Second Edition. . . . . Extra fcap. 8vo. 1s. 6d.

Tancock. *An English Grammar and Reading Book,* for Lower
Forms in Classical Schools. By O. W. TANCOCK, M.A. *Fourth Edition.*
Extra fcap. 8vo. 3s. 6d.

Earle. *The Philology of the English Tongue.* By J. EARLE, M.A.,
Professor of Anglo-Saxon. *Third Edition.* . . Extra fcap. 8vo. 7s. 6d.

Earle. *A Book for the Beginner in Anglo-Saxon.* By the same Author.
Third Edition. . . . . Extra fcap. 8vo. 2s. 6d.

Sweet. *An Anglo-Saxon Primer, with Grammar, Notes, and Glossary.*
By HENRY SWEET, M.A. *Third Edition.* . . Extra fcap. 8vo. 2s. 6d.

Sweet. *An Anglo-Saxon Reader.* In Prose and Verse. With Grammatical Introduction, Notes, and Glossary. By the same Author. *Fourth
Edition, Revised and Enlarged.* . . . . Extra fcap. 8vo. 8s. 6d.

LIST OF SCHOOL BOOKS. 7

Sweet. *Anglo-Saxon Reading Primers.*
  I. *Selected Homilies of Ælfric.* . Extra fcap. 8vo. *stiff covers*, 1s. 6d.
  II. *Extracts from Alfred's Orosius.* Extra fcap. 8vo. *stiff covers*, 1s. 6d.

Sweet. *First Middle English Primer, with Grammar and Glossary.*
By the same Author. . . . . Extra fcap. 8vo. 2s.

Morris and Skeat. *Specimens of Early English.* A New and Revised Edition. With Introduction, Notes, and Glossarial Index. By R. MORRIS, LL.D., and W. W. SKEAT, M.A.
  Part I. From Old English Homilies to King Horn (A.D. 1150 to A.D. 1300). *Second Edition.* . . . . . . Extra fcap. 8vo. 9s.
  Part II. From Robert of Gloucester to Gower (A.D. 1298 to A.D. 1393). *Second Edition.* . . . . Extra fcap. 8vo. 7s. 6d.

Skeat. *Specimens of English Literature,* from the 'Ploughmans Crede' to the 'Shepheardes Calender' (A.D. 1394 to A.D. 1579). With Introduction, Notes, and Glossarial Index. By W. W. SKEAT, M.A.
Extra fcap. 8vo. 7s. 6d.

Typical Selections from the best English Writers, with Introductory Notices. *Second Edition.* In Two Volumes. Vol. I. Latimer to Berkeley. Vol. II. Pope to Macaulay. . . Extra fcap. 8vo. 3s. 6d. each.

A SERIES OF ENGLISH CLASSICS.—

Langland. *The Vision of William concerning Piers the Plowman,* by WILLIAM LANGLAND. Edited by W. W. SKEAT, M.A. *Third Edition.*
Extra fcap. 8vo. 4s. 6d.

Chaucer. I. *The Prologue to the Canterbury Tales; The Knightes Tale; The Nonne Prestes Tale.* Edited by R. MORRIS, LL.D. *Fifty-first Thousand.* . . . . Extra fcap. 8vo. 2s. 6d.

Chaucer. II. *The Prioresses Tale; Sir Thopas; The Monkes Tale; The Clerkes Tale; The Squieres Tale, &c.* Edited by W. W. SKEAT, M.A. *Second Edition.* . . . . Extra fcap. 8vo. 4s. 6d.

Chaucer. III. *The Tale of the Man of Lawe; The Pardoneres Tale; The Second Nonnes Tale; The Chanouns Yemannes Tale:* By the same Editor. *Second Edition.* . . . . . Extra fcap. 8vo. 4s. 6d.

Gamelyn, The Tale of. Edited by W. W. SKEAT, M.A.
Extra fcap. 8vo. *stiff covers*, 1s. 6d.

Wycliffe. *The New Testament in English,* according to the Version by JOHN WYCLIFFE, about A.D. 1380, and Revised by JOHN PURVEY, about A.D. 1388. With Introduction and Glossary by W. W. SKEAT, M.A.
Extra fcap. 8vo. 6s.

Wycliffe. *The Books of Job, Psalms, Proverbs, Ecclesiastes, and the Song of Solomon:* according to the Wycliffite Version made by NICHOLAS DE HEREFORD, about A.D. 1381, and Revised by JOHN PURVEY, about A.D. 1388. With Introduction and Glossary by W. W. SKEAT, M.A. Extra fcap. 8vo. 3s. 6d.

Spenser. *The Faery Queene.* Books I and II. Edited by G. W. KITCHIN, D.D.
  Book I. *Tenth Edition.* . . . . . Extra fcap. 8vo. 2s. 6d.
  Book II. *Sixth Edition.* . . . . . Extra fcap. 8vo. 2s. 6d.

Hooker. *Ecclesiastical Polity.* Book I. Edited by R. W. CHURCH, M.A., Dean of St. Paul's. *Second Edition.* . . . Extra fcap. 8vo. 2s.

Marlowe and Greene.—MARLOWE'S *Tragical History of Dr. Faustus,* and GREENE'S *Honourable History of Friar Bacon and Friar Bungay.* Edited by A. W. WARD, M.A. . . . . . Extra fcap. 8vo. 5s. 6d.

Marlowe. *Edward II.* Edited by O. W. TANCOCK, M.A.
Extra fcap. 8vo. 3s.

Shakespeare. Select Plays. Edited by W. G. CLARK, M.A., and W. ALDIS WRIGHT, M.A. . . . . . Extra fcap. 8vo. *stiff covers.*

The Merchant of Venice. 1s.   *Macbeth.* 1s. 6d.
Richard the Second. 1s. 6d.   *Hamlet.* 2s.

Edited by W. ALDIS WRIGHT, M.A.

The Tempest. 1s. 6d.   *Coriolanus.* 2s. 6d.
As You Like It. 1s. 6d.   *Richard the Third.* 2s. 6d.
A Midsummer Night's Dream. 1s. 6d.   *Henry the Fifth.* 2s.
Twelfth Night. 1s. 6d.   *King John.* 1s. 6d. *Just Published.*
Julius Cæsar. 2s.   *King Lear.* 1s. 6d.

Shakespeare as a Dramatic Artist; *a popular Illustration of the Principles of Scientific Criticism.* By RICHARD G. MOULTON, M.A.
Crown 8vo. 5s.

Bacon. I. *Advancement of Learning.* Edited by W. ALDIS WRIGHT, M.A. *Second Edition.* . . . . . . Extra fcap. 8vo. 4s. 6d.

Bacon. II. *The Essays.* With Introduction and Notes. *In Preparation.*

Milton. I. *Areopagitica.* With Introduction and Notes. By JOHN W. HALES, M.A. *Third Edition.* . . . . Extra fcap. 8vo. 3s.

Milton. II. *Poems.* Edited by R. C. BROWNE, M.A. 2 vols. *Fifth Edition.* . . Extra fcap. 8vo. 6s. 6d. Sold separately, Vol. I. 4s.; Vol. II. 3s.

In paper covers:—
Lycidas, 3d.   *L'Allegro,* 3d.   *Il Penseroso,* 4d.   *Comus,* 6d.
Samson Agonistes, 6d.

Milton. III. *Samson Agonistes.* Edited with Introduction and Notes by JOHN CHURTON COLLINS. . . . Extra fcap. 8vo. *stiff covers,* 1s.

Bunyan. I. *The Pilgrim's Progress, Grace Abounding, Relation of the Imprisonment of Mr. John Bunyan.* Edited, with Biographical Introduction and Notes, by E. VENABLES, M.A. . . . Extra fcap. 8vo. 5s.

Bunyan. II. *Holy War, &c.* By the same Editor. *In the Press.*

Dryden. *Select Poems.*—*Stanzas on the Death of Oliver Cromwell; Astræa Redux; Annus Mirabilis; Absalom and Achitophel; Religio Laici; The Hind and the Panther.* Edited by W. D. CHRISTIE, M.A.
Extra fcap. 8vo. 3s. 6d.

LIST OF SCHOOL BOOKS. 9

Locke's *Conduct of the Understanding.* Edited, with Introduction, Notes, &c. by T. FOWLER, M.A. *Second Edition.* . . Extra fcap. 8vo. 2s.

Addison. *Selections from Papers in the 'Spectator.'* With Notes. By T. ARNOLD, M.A. . . . . . . Extra fcap. 8vo. 4s. 6d.

Steele. *Selected Essays from the Tatler, Spectator, and Guardian.* By AUSTIN DOBSON. . . Extra fcap. 8vo. 5s. *In white Parchment,* 7s. 6d.

Berkeley. *Select Works of Bishop Berkeley,* with an Introduction and Notes, by A. C. FRASER, LL.D. *Third Edition.* . . Crown 8vo. 7s. 6d.

Pope. I. *Essay on Man.* Edited by MARK PATTISON, B.D. *Sixth Edition.* . . . . Extra fcap. 8vo. 1s. 6d.

Pope. II. *Satires and Epistles.* By the same Editor. *Second Edition.* Extra fcap. 8vo. 2s.

Parnell. *The Hermit.* . . . . . *Paper covers,* 2d.

Johnson. I. *Rasselas; Lives of Dryden and Pope.* Edited by ALFRED MILNES, M.A. . . . . . Extra fcap. 8vo. 4s. 6d.
Lives of Pope and Dryden. . . . . . *Stiff covers,* 2s. 6d.

Johnson. II. *Vanity of Human Wishes.* With Notes, by E. J. PAYNE, M.A. . . . . *Paper covers,* 4d.

Gray. *Selected Poems.* Edited by EDMUND GOSSE.
Extra fcap. 8vo. *Stiff covers,* 1s. 6d. *In white Parchment,* 3s.

Gray. *Elegy, and Ode on Eton College.* . . *Paper covers,* 2d.

Goldsmith. *The Deserted Village.* . . . *Paper covers,* 2d.

Cowper. I. *The Didactic Poems of* 1782, with Selections from the Minor Pieces, A.D. 1779-1783. Edited by H. T. GRIFFITH, B.A.
Extra fcap. 8vo. 3s.

Cowper. II. *The Task, with Tirocinium,* and Selections from the Minor Poems, A.D. 1784-1799. By the same Editor. *Second Edition.*
Extra fcap. 8vo. 3s.

Burke. I. *Thoughts on the Present Discontents; the two Speeches on America.* Edited by E. J. PAYNE, M.A. *Second Edition.*
Extra fcap. 8vo. 4s. 6d.

Burke. II. *Reflections on the French Revolution.* By the same Editor. *Second Edition.* . . . . . Extra fcap. 8vo. 5s.

Burke. III. *Four Letters on the Proposals for Peace with the Regicide Directory of France.* By the same Editor. *Second Edition.*
Extra fcap. 8vo. 5s.

Keats. *Hyperion,* Book I. With Notes, by W. T. ARNOLD, B.A.
Paper covers, 4d.

Byron. *Childe Harold.* With Introduction and Notes, by H. F. Tozer, M.A. Extra fcap. 8vo. Cloth, 3s. 6d. In White Parchment, 5s. *Just Published.*

Scott. *Lay of the Last Minstrel.* Introduction and Canto I, with Preface and Notes by W. Minto, M.A. . . . . *Paper covers,* 6d.

FRENCH AND ITALIAN.

Brachet. *Etymological Dictionary of the French Language,* with a Preface on the Principles of French Etymology. Translated into English by G. W. Kitchin, D.D., Dean of Winchester. *Third Edition.*
Crown 8vo. 7s. 6d.

Brachet. *Historical Grammar of the French Language.* Translated into English by G. W. Kitchin, D.D. *Fourth Edition.*
Extra fcap. 8vo. 3s. 6d.

Saintsbury. *Primer of French Literature.* By George Saintsbury, M.A. *Second Edition.* . .. . . . Extra fcap. 8vo. 2s.

Saintsbury. *Short History of French Literature.* By the same Author. . . . . Crown 8vo. 10s. 6d.

Saintsbury. *Specimens of French Literature.* Crown 8vo. 9s.

Beaumarchais. *Le Barbier de Séville.* With Introduction and Notes by Austin Dobson. . . . . . . Extra fcap. 8vo. 2s. 6d.

Blouët. *L'Éloquence de la Chaire et de la Tribune Françaises.* Edited by Paul Blouët, B.A. (Univ. Gallic.). Vol. I. *French Sacred Oratory.*
Extra fcap. 8vo. 2s. 6d.

Corneille. *Horace.* With Introduction and Notes by George Saintsbury, M.A. . . , . . . Extra fcap. 8vo. 2s. 6d.

Corneille. *Cinna.* { In one volume, with Introduction and
Molière. *Les Femmes Savantes.* { Notes by Gustave Masson, B.A.
Extra fcap. 8vo. 2s. 6d.

Masson. *Louis XIV and his Contemporaries;* as described in Extracts from the best Memoirs of the Seventeenth Century. With English Notes, Genealogical Tables, &c. By Gustave Masson, B.A. Extra fcap. 8vo. 2s. 6d.

Molière. *Les Précieuses Ridicules.* With Introduction and Notes by Andrew Lang, M.A. . . . . . Extra fcap. 8vo. 1s. 6d.

Molière. *Les Fourberies de Scapin.* { With Voltaire's Life of Molière. By
Racine. *Athalie.* { Gustave Masson, B.A.
Extra fcap. 8vo. 2s. 6d.

Molière. *Les Fourberies de Scapin.* With Voltaire's Life of Molière. By Gustave Masson, B.A. . . Extra fcap. 8vo. *stiff covers,* 1s. 6d.

Musset. *On ne badine pas avec l'Amour,* and *Fantasio.* With Introduction, Notes, etc., by Walter Herries Pollock. Extra fcap. 8vo. 2s.

LIST OF SCHOOL BOOKS.

NOVELETTES :—

Xavier de Maistre. *Voyage autour de ma Chambre.*　⎫　By Gustave
Madame de Duras. *Ourika.*　　　　　　　　　　　　　　　⎪　Masson, B.A.
Piévée. *La Dot de Suzette.*　　　　　　　　　　　　　　⎬　2nd Edition.
Edmond About. *Les Jumeaux de l'Hôtel Corneille.*　⎪　Ext. fcap. 8vo.
Rodolphe Töpffer. *Mésaventures d'un Écolier.*　　　⎭　2s. 6d.

Quinet. *Lettres à sa Mère.* Edited by G. Saintsbury, M.A.
　　　　　　　　　　　　　　　　　　　　　　　　　Extra fcap. 8vo. 2s.

Racine. *Andromaque.*　⎫ With Louis Racine's Life of his Father. By
Corneille. *Le Menteur.*　⎭ Gustave Masson, B.A.
　　　　　　　　　　　　　　　　　　　　　　　Extra fcap. 8vo. 2s. 6d.

Regnard. . . . *Le Joueur.*　⎫ By Gustave Masson, B.A.
Brueys and Palaprat. *Le Grondeur.*　⎭ Extra fcap. 8vo. 2s. 6d.

Sainte-Beuve. *Selections from the Causeries du Lundi.* Edited by
G. Saintsbury, M.A.. . . . . Extra fcap. 8vo. 2s.

Sévigné. *Selections from the Correspondence of* **Madame de Sévigné**
and her chief Contemporaries. Intended more especially for Girls' Schools. By
Gustave Masson, B.A. . . . . . Extra fcap. 8vo. 3s.

Voltaire. *Mérope.* Edited by G. Saintsbury, M.A. Extra fcap. 8vo. 2s.

Dante. *Selections from the 'Inferno.'* With Introduction and Notes,
by H. B. Cotterill, B.A. . . . . . Extra fcap. 8vo. 4s. 6d.

Tasso. *La Gerusalemme Liberata.* Cantos i, ii. With Introduction
and Notes, by the same Editor. . . . . Extra fcap. 8vo. 2s. 6d.

GERMAN, &c.

Buchheim. *Modern German Reader.* A Graduated Collection of
Extracts in Prose and Poetry from Modern German writers. Edited by C. A.
Buchheim, Phil. Doc.
　Part I. With English Notes, a Grammatical Appendix, and a complete
　Vocabulary. *Fourth Edition.* . . . . Extra fcap. 8vo. 2s. 6d.
　Part II. With English Notes and an Index. Extra fcap. 8vo. 2s. 6d. *Just
　Published.*
　Part III. In preparation.

Lange. *The Germans at Home*; a Practical Introduction to German
Conversation, with an Appendix containing the Essentials of German Grammar.
By Hermann Lange. *Second Edition.* . . . . . 8vo. 2s. 6d.

Lange. *The German Manual*; a German Grammar, a Reading
Book, and a Handbook of German Conversation. By the same Author.
　　　　　　　　　　　　　　　　　　　　　　　　　8vo. 7s. 6d.

Lange. *A Grammar of the German Language,* being a reprint of the
Grammar contained in *The German Manual.* By the same Author. 8vo. 3s. 6d.

Lange. *German Composition*; a Theoretical and Practical Guide to
the Art of Translating English Prose into German. By the same Author.
　　　　　　　　　　　　　　　　　　　　　　　　　8vo. 4s. 6d.

CLARENDON PRESS

Goethe. *Egmont.* With a Life of Goethe, etc. Edited by C. A. BUCHHEIM, Phil. Doc. *Third Edition.* . . . Extra fcap. 8vo. 3s.

Goethe. *Iphigenie auf Tauris.* A Drama. With a Critical Introduction and Notes. Edited by C. A. BUCHHEIM, Phil. Doc. *Second Edition.*
Extra fcap. 8vo. 3s.

Heine's *Prosa,* being Selections from his Prose Works. Edited with English Notes, etc., by C. A. BUCHHEIM, Phil. Doc. Extra fcap. 8vo. 4s. 6d.

Lessing. *Laokoon.* With Introduction, Notes, etc. By A. HAMANN, Phil. Doc., M.A. . . . . Extra fcap. 8vo. 4s. 6d.

Lessing. *Minna von Barnhelm.* A Comedy. With a Life of Lessing, Critical Analysis, Complete Commentary, etc. Edited by C. A. BUCHHEIM, Phil. Doc. *Fourth Edition.* . . Extra fcap. 8vo. 3s. 6d.

Lessing. *Nathan der Weise.* With English Notes, etc. Edited by C. A. BUCHHEIM, Phil. Doc. . . . . . Extra fcap. 8vo. 4s. 6d.

Schiller's *Historische Skizzen:—Egmonts Leben und Tod,* and *Belagerung von Antwerpen.* Edited by C. A. BUCHHEIM, Phil. Doc. *Third Edition, Revised and Enlarged, with a Map.* . Extra fcap. 8vo. 2s. 6d.

Schiller. *Wilhelm Tell.* With a Life of Schiller; an Historical and Critical Introduction, Arguments, a Complete Commentary, and Map. Edited by C. A. BUCHHEIM, Phil. Doc. *Sixth Edition.* . Extra fcap. 8vo. 3s. 6d.

Schiller. *Wilhelm Tell.* Edited by C. A. BUCHHEIM, Phil. Doc. *School Edition.* With Map. . . . . . Extra fcap. 8vo. 2s.

Schiller. *Wilhelm Tell.* Translated into English Verse by E. MASSIE, M.A. . . . . Extra fcap. 8vo. 5s.

GOTHIC AND ICELANDIC.

Skeat. *The Gospel of St. Mark in Gothic.* Edited by W. W. SKEAT, M.A. . . . . Extra fcap. 8vo. 4s.

Vigfusson and Powell. *An Icelandic Prose Reader,* with Notes, Grammar, and Glossary. By GUDBRAND VIGFUSSON, M.A., and F. YORK POWELL, M.A. . . . . Extra fcap. 8vo. 10s. 6d.

MATHEMATICS AND PHYSICAL SCIENCE.

Hamilton and Ball. *Book-keeping.* By Sir R. G. C. HAMILTON, K.C.B., Under-Secretary for Ireland, and JOHN BALL (of the firm of Quilter, Ball, & Co.). *New and Enlarged Edition* . . . Extra fcap. 8vo. 2s.

Hensley. *Figures made Easy: a first Arithmetic Book.* By LEWIS HENSLEY, M.A. . . . . Crown 8vo. 6d.

Hensley. *Answers to the Examples in Figures made Easy,* together with 2000 additional Examples formed from the Tables in the same, with Answers. By the same Author. . . . . . Crown 8vo. 1s.

LIST OF SCHOOL BOOKS. 13

Hensley. *The Scholar's Arithmetic;* with Answers to the Examples.
By the same Author. . . . . Crown 8vo. 4s. 6d.
Hensley. *The Scholar's Algebra.* An Introductory work on Algebra.
By the same Author. . . . . Crown 8vo. 4s. 6d.

Baynes. *Lessons on Thermodynamics.* By R. E. BAYNES, M.A.,
Lee's Reader in Physics. . . . . Crown 8vo. 7s. 6d.
Donkin. *Acoustics.* By W. F. DONKIN, M.A., F.R.S. *Second Edition.*
Crown 8vo. 7s. 6d.
Euclid Revised. Containing the essentials of the Elements of Plane
Geometry as given by Euclid in his First Six Books. Edited by R. C. J. NIXON,
M.A., Formerly Scholar of St. Peter's College, Cambridge.
Crown 8vo. *Nearly ready.*
Harcourt and Madan. *Exercises in Practical Chemistry.* Vol. I.
Elementary Exercises. By A. G. VERNON HARCOURT, M.A.; and H. G.
MADAN, M.A. *Third Edition.* Revised by H. G. Madan, M.A.
Crown 8vo. 9s.
Madan. *Tables of Qualitative Analysis.* Arranged by H. G. MADAN,
M.A. . . . . Large 4to. 4s. 6d.
Maxwell. *An Elementary Treatise on Electricity.* By J. CLERK
MAXWELL, M.A., F.R.S. Edited by W. GARNETT, M.A. Demy 8vo. 7s. 6d.
Stewart. *A Treatise on Heat,* with numerous Woodcuts and Diagrams. By BALFOUR STEWART, LL.D., F.R.S., Professor of Natural Philosophy
in Owens College, Manchester. *Fourth Edition.* . Extra fcap. 8vo. 7s. 6d.
Vernon-Harcourt. *A Treatise on Rivers and Canals,* relating to
the Control and Improvement of Rivers, and the Design, Construction, and
Development of Canals. By LEVESON FRANCIS VERNON-HARCOURT, M.A.,
M.I.C.E. 2 vols. (Vol. I, Text. Vol. II, Plates.) . . . 8vo. 21s.
Vernon-Harcourt. *Harbours and Docks;* their Physical Features,
History, Construction, Equipment, and Maintenance. By the same Author.
2 vols. (Vol. I, Text. Vol. II Plates.) . . . . . 8vo. 25s.
Williamson. *Chemistry for Students.* By A. W. WILLIAMSON,
Phil. Doc., F.R.S., Professor of Chemistry, University College London. *A new
Edition with Solutions.* . . . . . . Extra fcap. 8vo. 8s. 6d.

HISTORY, &c.

Freeman. *A Short History of the Norman Conquest of England.*
By E. A. FREEMAN, M.A. *Second Edition.* . Extra fcap. 8vo. 2s. 6d.
George. *Genealogical Tables illustrative of Modern History.* By
H. B. GEORGE, M.A. *Second Edition, Revised and Enlarged.* Small 4to. 12s.
Kitchin. *A History of France.* With Numerous Maps, Plans, and
Tables. By G. W. KITCHIN. D.D., Dean of Winchester. *Second Edition.*
Vol. 1. To the Year 1453. . . . . 10s. 6d.
Vol. 2. From 1453 to 1624. . . . . . . 10s. 6d.
Vol. 3. From 1624 to 1793. . . . . . . 10s. 6d.

/ 4   CLARENDON PRESS SCHOOL LIST.

Rawlinson. *A Manual of Ancient History.* By GEORGE RAW-
LINSON, M.A., Camden Professor of Ancient History. *Second Edition.*
Demy 8vo. 14s.

Rogers. *A Manual of Political Economy,* for the use of Schools.
By J. E. THOROLD ROGERS, M.P. *Third Edition.* Extra fcap. 8vo. 4s. 6d.

Stubbs. *The Constitutional History of England, in its Origin and
Development.* By WILLIAM STUBBS, D.D., Lord Bishop of Chester. Three
vols. . . . . Crown 8vo. each 12s.

Stubbs. *Select Charters and other Illustrations of English Constitutional History,* from the Earliest Times to the Reign of Edward I.
Arranged and edited by W. STUBBS, D.D. *Fourth Edition,* Crown 8vo. 8s. 6d.

Stubbs. *Magna Carta:* a careful reprint. . . . 4to. *stitched,* 1s.

ART.

Hullah. *The Cultivation of the Speaking Voice.* By JOHN HULLAH.
Extra fcap. 8vo. 2s. 6d.

Maclaren. *A System of Physical Education: Theoretical and Prac-
tical.* With 346 Illustrations drawn by A. MACDONALD, of the Oxford School of
Art. By ARCHIBALD MACLAREN, the Gymnasium, Oxford. *Second Edition.*
Extra fcap. 8vo. 7s. 6d.

Troutbeck and Dale. *A Music Primer for Schools.* By J. TROUT-
BECK, M.A., Music Master in Westminster School, and R. F. DALE, M.A.,
B. Mus., Assistant Master in Westminster School. . Crown 8vo. 1s. 6d.

Tyrwhitt. *A Handbook of Pictorial Art.* By R. St. J. TYRWHITT,
M.A. With coloured Illustrations, Photographs, and a chapter on Perspective
by A. MACDONALD. *Second Edition.* . . . 8vo. *half morocco,* 18s.

Student's Handbook to the University and Colleges of Oxford.
Eighth Edition. . . . . Extra fcap. 8vo. 2s. 6d.

Helps to the Study of the Bible, taken from the *Oxford Bible for
Teachers,* comprising Summaries of the several Books, with copious Explanatory
Notes and Tables illustrative of Scripture History and the Characteristics of
Bible Lands; with a complete Index of Subjects, a Concordance, a Dictionary
of Proper Names, and a series of Maps. . . . Crown 8vo. 3s. 6d.

☞ *All communications relating to Books included in this List, and
offers of new Books and new Editions, should be addressed to*

THE SECRETARY TO THE DELEGATES,
CLARENDON PRESS,
OXFORD.

BOOKS FOR SCHOOL LIBRARIES.

An Etymological Dictionary of
the English Language, arranged on
an Historical Basis. By W. W. SKEAT,
M.A. Second Edition. 2*l.* 4*s.*

Shakespeare as a Dramatic Artist. By R. G. MOULTON, M.A. 5*s.*

English Plant Names, from
the tenth to the fifteenth Century. By
J. EARLE, M.A. 5*s.*

Baedae Historia Ecclesiastica.
Edited by G. H. MOBERLY, M.A.
10*s.* 6*d.*

Chapters of Early English
Church History. By W. BRIGHT,
D.D. 12*s.*

History of the Norman Conquest of England: its Causes and Results. By E. A. FREEMAN, D.C.L.
In 6 vols. 5*l.* 9*s.* 6*d.*

The Reign of William Rufus
and the Accession of Henry the First.
By E. A. FREEMAN, D.C.L. In 2 vols.
1*l.* 16*s.*

Fuller's Church History of
Britain. Edited by J. S. BREWER,
M.A. In 6 vols. 1*l.* 19*s.*

Burnet's History of the Reformation of the Church of England.
New Edition, revised by N. POCOCK,
M.A. In 7 vols. 1*l.* 10*s.*

Clarendon's History of the
Rebellion and Civil Wars in England,
together with his Life, including a
Continuation of his History. 1*l.* 2*s.*

A History of England, principally in the Seventeenth Century.
Translation edited by G. W. KITCHIN,
D.D., and C. W. BOASE, M.A. In
6 vols. 3*l.* 3*s.*

A History of Greece, B.C. 146
to A.D. 1864. By GEORGE FINLAY,
LL.D. New Edition, by H. F. TOZER,
M.A. In 7 vols. 3*l.* 10*s.*

Italy and her Invaders. By
T. HODGKIN, M.A. Vols. I-IV. 3*l.* 8*s.*

Some Account of the Church in
the Apostolic Age. By W. W. SHIRLEY,
D.D. Second Edition. 3*s.* 6*d.*

Pearson's Exposition of the
Creed. Revised and corrected by E.
BURTON, D.D. Sixth Edition. 10*s.* 6*d.*

Hooker's Works: the text as
arranged by JOHN KEBLE, M.A. In
2 vols. 11*s.*

Bacon's Novum Organum.
Edited by T. FOWLER, M.A. 14*s.*

Scherer. A History of German
Literature. Translated from the Third
German Edition by Mrs. F. CONYBEARE.
Edited by F. MAX MÜLLER. 2 vols.
21*s.* *Just Published.*

A Course of Lectures on Art.
By J. RUSKIN, M.A. 6*s.*

Aspects of Poetry. By J. C.
SHAIRP, M.A. 10*s.* 6*d.*

Geology of Oxford and the
Valley of the Thames. By JOHN
PHILLIPS, M.A., F.R.S. 1*l.* 1*s.*

BOOKS FOR SCHOOL LIBRARIES.

A Handbook of Descriptive Astronomy. By G. F. CHAMBERS, F.R.A.S. Third Edition. 1*l*. 8*s*.

A Cycle of Celestial Objects. By Admiral W. H. SMYTH, R.N. Revised ,etc. by G. F. CHAMBERS, F.R.A.S. 12*s*.

British Barrows: a Record of the Examination of Sepulchral Mounds in various Parts of England. By W. GREENWELL, M.A., F.S.A. With Appendix, &c. by G. ROLLESTON, M.D., F.R.S. 25*s*.

A Treatise on Rivers and Canals. By L. F. VERNON-HARCOURT, M.A. 2 vols. 21*s*.

Harbours and Docks. By L. F. VERNON-HARCOURT, M.A. 2 vols. 25*s*.

Fragments and Specimens of Early Latin. By J. WORDSWORTH, M.A. 18*s*.

The Roman Poets of the Republic. By W. Y. SELLAR, M.A. 14*s*.

The Roman Poets of the Augustan Age. Virgil. By W. Y. SELLAR, M.A. 9*s*.

Lectures and Essays on Subjects connected with Latin Literature and Scholarship. By H. NETTLESHIP, M.A. 7*s*. 6*d*.

Catullus, a Commentary on. By ROBINSON ELLIS, M.A. 16*s*.

Selections from the less known Latin Poets. By NORTH PINDER, M.A. 15*s*.

A Grammar of the Homeric Dialect. By D. B. MONRO, M.A. 10*s*. 6*d*.

A Manual of Greek Historical Inscriptions. By E. L. HICKS, M.A. 10*s*. 6*d*.

Plato: The Dialogues. Translated into English, with an Analysis and Introduction, by B. JOWETT, M.A. 3*l*. 10*s*.

Thucydides. Translated into English, with Introduction, Marginal Analysis, Notes, and Indices, by B. JOWETT, M.A. 1*l*. 12*s*.

A New English Dictionary on Historical Principles. Founded mainly on the materials collected by the Philological Society. Edited by JAMES A. H. MURRAY, LL.D. Part I. A—ANT. Part II. ANT—BATTEN. 12*s*. 6*d*. each.

London: HENRY FROWDE,

OXFORD UNIVERSITY PRESS WAREHOUSE, AMEN CORNER.

Edinburgh : 6, QUEEN STREET.

Oxford : CLARENDON PRESS DEPOSITORY,

116, HIGH STREET.

PR   Gray, Thomas
3501   Selected poems
G67

PLEASE DO NOT REMOVE
CARDS OR SLIPS FROM THIS POCKET

UNIVERSITY OF TORONTO LIBRARY

www.ingramcontent.com/pod-product-compliance
Lightning Source LLC
Chambersburg PA
CBHW030311170426
43202CB00009B/963